Who Needs Nature?

Perception in Communication

WHO NEEDS NATURE?

EDITED BY *Dixie S. Jackson*

*University of Illinois
at Urbana*

JOHN WILEY & SONS, INC.
NEW YORK · LONDON · SYDNEY · TORONTO

cover: AIA/American Institute of Architects. Used by permission.

Library of Congress Cataloging in Publication Data:

Jackson, Dixie S   comp.
  Who needs nature?

  (Perception in communication)
  1. College readers.   2. Human ecology—Literary collections.   I. Title.

PE1122.J27   808'.04275   72–6788
ISBN 0–471–43150–8

Printed in the United States of America

10 9 8 7 6 5 4 3 2 1

Series Preface

"Perception in Communication" is a series of brief topical readers presenting a collection of expository prose, verse, fiction, drama, and nonverbal media for the student of composition. No restrictive framework has been imposed on any of the volumes. If a common framework exists, it stems from the editors' emphasis on the principle of comparison and contrast and their mutual desire to make the questions and exercises participatory. The questions are focused on themes and matters of rhetorical technique that will provoke discussion between instructor and student in responses to the authors and editors.

Experience demonstrates that a student tends to write better when a timely, substantial subject engages his interest, or when the subject is elaborated and reviewed in a variety of modes of communication. Although the major emphasis of this series is on written communication, there are also a number of multimedia projects such as collages, comic routines, poems, dramatic productions, films, pictorial essays, posters, songs, and tapes. The editors use this multimedia material in such a manner that they are very definitely assignments in composition.

By acknowledging several modes of communication and encouraging experimentation in more than one, the editors recognize the heterogeneity of today's college audience and its various commitments, concerns, goals, and needs. It is the editors' belief that presenting these various modes of communication will engage not only the reader's mind but also his sensory perception.

CHARLES SANDERS

University of Illinois at Urbana

Preface

Today we cannot read a newspaper or hear a newscast without being reminded that our nation is in an environmental crisis. Often we are irritated by the reports; at times we are alarmed. "Why don't the engineers or the scientists come up with a solution to this problem?" we wonder. "Why doesn't the government pass laws to halt environmental abuses? Why did they let this crisis develop?"

But the environmental crisis is not of someone else's making. Each of us has contributed to it through a life style that makes insupportable demands on earth's resources.

This anthology investigates the attitudes and actions from which the environmental crisis has grown. The selections describe our physical and emotional needs for a natural environment. They discuss our failure to recognize the intricate structure of the biotic community. Some articles investigate the economic priorities that motivate us to alter our environment despite dangerous consequences to ourselves. Others condemn our concern for private over public good. Many expose the outmoded bureaucracies, short-sighted goals, and aesthetic poverty that have led us to convert this once-lovely land into ugly cities, monotonous suburbs, litter-strewn highways, and scarred countrysides. Several condemn our relentless production of new humans who, nurtured with values like our own, endlessly multiply our assaults on the land. Most selections urge us to reassess our values and to restore our environment.

Our success in rebuilding a pleasing environment will depend partly on effective communication with others. To reach the widest possible audience, we must learn to use effectively all forms of communication; we cannot depend only on verbal messages. There is, therefore, a strong bond between this anthology and a course designed to teach those communication skills. This book includes a variety of selections—drawings, cartoons, advertisements, photographs, poems, and the lyrics from a popular song, as well as essays, a speech, and a narrative. Through these works the text explores forms of communication available to the student. The assignments and projects encourage him to use these forms and to experiment with others.

In the world outside the college classroom a person writes no "themes." Instead, motivated by a purpose, he communicates—in an angry letter, a moving poem, or a striking painting. He researches because he wants to know more about a topic. He writes a report because he possesses information important to others. In using this textbook, the student does not write themes either. Instead, he engages in meaningful communication about a problem: the environmental crisis. The text suggests letters to write, a photographic essay to arrange, and testimony to prepare for city council hearings. It invites students to plan a model city or to create a drama. It suggests topics for further investigation and lists titles of pertinent books and articles to read.

The selections are arranged in three parts: "Our Attitudes," "Our Actions," and "The Outcome." Perhaps some selections consider topics about which you have given much thought. Others raise issues that you have not considered. After you have read the selections, you are encouraged to reexperience them, since a particular selection may give you new insights into another.

This brief text can touch only lightly on so complex an issue as the environmental crisis. But by being aware of the ideas introduced here, and by improving your ability to communicate effectively about them, you will be prepared to help resolve that crisis.

DIXIE S. JACKSON

University of Illinois at Urbana, 1973

Contents

Who Needs Nature?

Part One

OUR ATTITUDES

1. We Have Met the Enemy and He Is Us

© 1970 Walt Kelly. Courtesy Publishers-Hall Syndicate.

2. from *Genesis*

*Be fruitful, and multiply, and replenish the earth and subdue it:
and have dominion over the fish of the sea, and over the fowl of the
air, and over every living thing that moveth upon the earth.*

King James Version of the Bible.

3. *Observations*

You ask me to plow the ground. Shall I take a knife and tear my mother's bosom? You ask me to dig for stone. Shall I dig under her skin for her bones? You ask me to cut grass and make hay and sell it and be rich like white men. But how dare I cut off my mother's hair?

Speech by Smohalla, the great Nez Percé Indian preacher. Reproduced by permission of the *American Anthropological Association*, from *Memoirs of the American Anthropological Association*, Vol. II, 1907–1915.

4. *from* **Cry the Beloved Country**

ALAN PATON

Stand unshod upon it, for the ground is holy, being even as it came from the Creator. Keep it, guard it, care for it, for it keeps men, guards men, cares for men. Destroy it and man is destroyed.

From *Cry the Beloved Country* by Alan Paton. Printed by permission of Charles Scribner's Sons.

5. The Land Ethic

ALDO LEOPOLD

When god-like Odysseus returned from the wars in Troy, he hanged all on one rope a dozen slave-girls of his household whom he suspected of misbehavior during his absence.

This hanging involved no question of propriety. The girls were property. The disposal of property was then, as now, a matter of expediency, not of right and wrong.

Concepts of right and wrong were not lacking from Odysseus' Greece: witness the fidelity of his wife through the long years before at last his black-prowed galleys clove the wine-dark seas for home. The ethical structure of that day covered wives, but had not yet been extended to human chattels. During the three thousand years which have since elapsed, ethical criteria have been extended to many fields of conduct, with corresponding shrinkages in those judged by expediency only.

The Ethical Sequence

This extension of ethics, so far studied only by philosophers, is actu-

From *A Sand County Almanac with other essays on conservation from Round River* by Aldo Leopold. Copyright © 1949, 1953, 1966 by Oxford University Press, Inc. Reprinted by permission.

ally a process in ecological evolution. Its sequences may be described in ecological as well as in philosophical terms. An ethic, ecologically, is a limitation on freedom of action in the struggle for existence. An ethic, philosophically, is a differentiation of social from anti-social conduct. These are two definitions of one thing. The thing has its origin in the tendency of interdependent individuals or groups to evolve modes of co-operation. The ecologist calls these symbioses. Politics and economics are advanced symbioses in which the original free-for-all competition has been replaced, in part, by co-operative mechanisms with an ethical content.

The complexity of co-operative mechanisms has increased with population density, and with the efficiency of tools. It was simpler, for example, to define the anti-social uses of sticks and stones in the days of the mastodons than of bullets and billboards in the age of motors.

The first ethics dealt with the relation between individuals; the Mosaic Decalogue is an example. Later accretions dealt with the relation between the individual and society. The Golden Rule tries to integrate the individual to society; democracy to integrate social organization to the individual.

There is as yet no ethic dealing with man's relation to land and to the animals and plants which grow upon it. Land, like Odysseus' slave-girls, is still property. The land-relation is still strictly economic, entailing privileges but not obligations.

The extension of ethics to this third element in human environment is, if I read the evidence correctly, an evolutionary possibility and an ecological necessity. It is the third step in a sequence. The first two have already been taken. Individual thinkers since the days of Ezekiel and Isaiah have asserted that the despoliation of land is not only inexpedient but wrong. Society, however, has not yet affirmed their belief. I regard the present conservation movement as the embryo of such an affirmation.

An ethic may be regarded as a mode of guidance for meeting ecological situations so new or intricate, or involving such deferred reactions, that the path of social expediency is not discernible to the average individual. Animal instincts are modes of guidance for the individual in meeting such situations. Ethics are possibly a kind of community instinct in-the-making.

The Community Concept

All ethics so far evolved rest upon a single premise: that the individual is a member of a community of interdependent parts. His instincts prompt him to compete for his place in that community, but his ethics prompt him also to co-operate (perhaps in order that there may be a place to compete for).

The land ethic simply enlarges the boundaries of the community to include soils, waters, plants, and animals, or collectively: the land.

This sounds simple: do we not already sing our love for and obligation to the land of the free and the home of the brave? Yes, but just what and whom do we love? Certainly not the soil, which we are sending helter-skelter downriver. Certainly not the waters, which we assume have no function except to turn turbines, float barges, and carry off sewage. Certainly not the plants, of which we exterminate whole communities without batting an eye. Certainly not the animals, of which we have already extirpated many of the largest and most beautiful species. A land ethic of course cannot prevent the alteration, management, and use of these 'resources,' but it does affirm their right to continued existence, and, at least in spots, their continued existence in a natural state.

In short, a land ethic changes the role of *Homo sapiens* from conqueror of the land-community to plain member and citizen of it. It implies respect for his fellow-members, and also respect for the community as such.

In human history, we have learned (I hope) that the conqueror role is eventually self-defeating. Why? Because it is implicit in such a role that the conqueror knows, *ex cathedra,* just what makes the community clock tick, and just what and who is valuable, and what and who is worthless, in community life. It always turns out that he knows neither, and this is why his conquests eventually defeat themselves.

In the biotic community, a parallel situation exists. Abraham knew exactly what the land was for: it was to drip milk and honey into Abraham's mouth. At the present moment, the assurance with which we regard this assumption is inverse to the degree of our education.

The ordinary citizen today assumes that science knows what makes the community clock tick; the scientist is equally sure that he does not. He knows that the biotic mechanism is so complex that its workings may never be fully understood.

That man is, in fact, only a member of a biotic team is shown by an ecological interpretation of history. Many historical events, hitherto explained solely in terms of human enterprise, were actually biotic interactions between people and land. The characteristics of the land determined the facts quite as potently as the characteristics of the men who lived on it.

Consider, for example, the settlement of the Mississippi valley. In the years following the Revolution, three groups were contending for its control: the native Indian, the French and English traders, and the American settlers. Historians wonder what would have happened if the English at Detroit had thrown a little more weight into the Indian side of those tipsy scales which decided the outcome of the colonial migration into the cane-lands of Kentucky. It is time now to ponder the fact that the cane-lands, when subjected to the particular mixture of forces represented by the cow, plow, fire, and axe of the pioneer, became bluegrass. What if the plant succession inherent in this dark and bloody ground had, under the impact of these forces, given us some worthless sedge, shrub, or weed? Would Boone and Kenton have held out? Would there have been any overflow into Ohio, Indiana, Illinois, and Missouri? Any Louisiana Purchase? Any transcontinental union of new states? Any Civil War?

Kentucky was one sentence in the drama of history. We are commonly told what the human actors in this drama tried to do, but we are seldom told that their success, or the lack of it, hung in large degree on the reaction of particular soils to the impact of the particular forces exerted by their occupancy. In the case of Kentucky, we do not even know where the bluegrass came from—whether it is a native species, or a stowaway from Europe.

Contrast the cane-lands with what hindsight tells us about the Southwest, where the pioneers were equally brave, resourceful, and persevering. The impact of occupancy here brought no bluegrass, or other plant fitted to withstand the bumps and buffetings of hard use. This region, when grazed by livestock, reverted through a series of more and more worthless grasses, shrubs, and weeds to a condition of unstable equilibrium. Each recession of plant types bred erosion; each increment to erosion bred a further recession of plants. The result today is a progressive and mutual deterioration, not only of plants and soils, but of the animal community subsisting thereon. The early settlers did not expect this: on the ciénegas of New Mexico some even cut ditches to hasten it. So subtle has been its progress that few residents of the region are aware of it. It is quite invisible to the tourist who finds this wrecked landscape colorful and charming (as indeed it is, but it bears scant resemblance to what it was in 1848).

This same landscape was "developed" once before, but with quite different results. The Pueblo Indians settled the Southwest in pre-Columbian times, but they happened *not* to be equipped with range livestock. Their civilization expired, but not because their land expired.

In India, regions devoid of any sod-forming grass have been settled, apparently without wrecking the land, by the simple expedient of carrying the grass to the cow, rather than vice versa. (Was this the result of some deep wisdom, or was it just good luck? I do not know.)

In short, the plant succession steered the course of history; the pioneer simply demonstrated, for good or ill, what successions inhered in the land. Is history taught in this spirit? It will be, once the concept of land as a community really penetrates our intellectual life.

The Ecological Conscience

Conservation is a state of harmony between men and land. Despite nearly a century of propaganda, conservation still proceeds at a snail's pace; progress still consists largely of letterhead pieties and convention oratory. On the back forty we still slip two steps backward for each forward stride.

The usual answer to this dilemma is "more conservation education." No one will debate this, but is it certain that only the *volume* of education needs stepping up? Is something lacking in the *content* as well?

It is difficult to give a fair summary of its content in brief form, but, as I understand it, the content is substantially this: obey the law, vote right, join some organizations, and practice what conservation is profitable on your own land; the government will do the rest.

Is not this formula too easy to accomplish anything worthwhile? It defines no right or wrong, assigns no obligation, calls for no sacrifice, implies no change in the current philosophy of values. In respect of land-use, it urges only enlightened self-interest. Just how far will such education take us? An example will perhaps yield a partial answer.

By 1930 it had become clear to all except the ecologically blind that southwestern Wisconsin's topsoil was slipping seaward. In 1933 the farmers were told that if they would adopt certain remedial practices for five years, the public would donate CCC labor to install them, plus the necessary machinery and materials. The offer was widely accepted, but the practices were widely forgotten when the five-year contract period was up. The farmers continued only those practices that yielded an immediate and visible economic gain for themselves.

This led to the idea that maybe farmers would learn more quickly if they themselves wrote the rules. Accordingly the Wisconsin Legislature in 1937 passed the Soil Conservation District Law. This said to farmers, in effect: *We, the public, will furnish you free technical service and loan you specialized machinery, if you will write your own rules for land-use. Each county may write its own rules, and these will have the force of law.* Nearly all the counties promptly organized to accept the proffered help, but after a decade of operation, *no county has yet written a single rule.* There has been visible progress in such practices as strip-cropping, pasture renovation, and soil liming, but none in fencing woodlots against grazing, and none in excluding plow and cow from steep slopes. The farmers, in short, have selected those remedial practices which were profitable anyhow, and ignored those which were profitable to the community, but not clearly profitable to themselves.

When one asks why no rules have been written, one is told that the community is not yet ready to support them; education must precede rules. But the education actually in progress makes no mention of obligations to land over and above those dictated by self-interest. The net result is that we have more education but less soil, fewer healthy woods, and as many floods as in 1937.

The puzzling aspect of such situations is that the existence of obligations over and above self-interest is taken for granted in such rural community enterprises as the betterment of roads, schools, churches, and baseball teams. Their existence is not taken for granted, nor as yet seriously discussed, in bettering the behavior of the water that falls on the land, or in the preserving of the beauty or diversity of the farm landscape. Land-use ethics are still governed wholly by economic self-interest, just as social ethics were a century ago.

To sum up: we asked the farmer to do what he conveniently could to save his soil, and he has done just that, and only that. The farmer who clears the woods off a 75 per cent slope, turns his cows into the clearing, and dumps its rainfall, rocks, and soil into the community creek, is still (if otherwise decent) a respected member of society. If he puts lime on his fields and plants his crops on contour, he is still entitled to all the privileges and emoluments of his Soil Conservation District. The District is a beautiful piece of social machinery, but it is coughing along on two cylinders because we have been too timid, and too anxious for quick success, to tell the farmer the true magnitude of his obligations. Obligations have no meaning without conscience, and the problem we face is the extension of the social conscience from people to land.

No important change in ethics was ever accomplished without an internal change in our intellectual emphasis, loyalties, affections, and convictions. The proof that conservation has not yet touched these foundations of conduct lies in the fact that philosophy and religion have not yet heard of it. In our attempt to make conservation easy, we have made it trivial.

Substitutes for A Land Ethic

When the logic of history hungers for bread and we hand out a stone, we are at pains to explain how much the stone resembles bread. I now describe some of the stones which serve in lieu of a land ethic.

One basic weakness in a conservation system based wholly on economic motives is that most members of the land community have no economic value. Wildflowers and songbirds are examples. Of the 22,000 higher plants and animals native to Wisconsin, it is doubtful whether more than 5 per cent can be sold, fed, eaten, or otherwise put to economic use. Yet these creatures are members of the biotic community, and if (as I believe) its stability depends on its integrity, they are entitled to continuance.

When one of these non-economic categories is threatened, and if we happen to love it, we invent subterfuges to give it economic importance. At the beginning of the century songbirds were supposed to be disappearing. Ornithologists jumped to the rescue with some distinctly shaky evidence to the effect that insects would eat us up if birds failed to control them. The evidence had to be economic in order to be valid.

It is painful to read these circumlocutions today. We have no land ethic yet, but we have at least drawn nearer the point of admitting that birds should continue as a matter of biotic right, regardless of the presence or absence of economic advantage to us.

A parallel situation exists in respect of predatory mammals, raptorial birds, and fish-eating birds. Time was when biologists somewhat overworked the evidence that these creatures preserve the health of game by killing weaklings, or that they control rodents for the farmer, or that they prey only on 'worthless' species. Here again, the evidence had to be economic in order to be valid. It is only in recent years that we hear the more honest argument that predators are members of the community, and that no special interest has the right to exterminate them for the sake of a benefit, real or fancied, to itself. Unfortunately this enlightened view is still in the talk stage. In the field the extermination of predators goes merrily on: witness the impending erasure of the timber wolf by fiat of Congress, the Conservation Bureaus, and many state legislatures.

Some species of trees have been "read out of the party" by economics-minded foresters because they grow too slowly, or have too low a sale value to pay as timber crops: white cedar, tamarack, cypress, beech, and hemlock are examples. In Europe, where forestry is ecologically more advanced, the non-commercial tree species are recognized as members of the native forest community, to be preserved as such, within reason. Moreover some (like beech) have been found to have a valuable function in building up soil fertility. The interdependence of the forest and its constituent tree species, ground flora, and fauna is taken for granted.

Lack of economic value is sometimes a character not only of species or groups, but of entire biotic communities: marshes, bogs, dunes, and "deserts" are examples. Our formula in such cases is to relegate their conservation to government as refuges, monuments, or parks. The difficulty is that these communities are usually interspersed with more valuable private lands; the government cannot possibly own or control such scattered parcels. The net effect is that we have relegated some of them to ultimate extinction over large areas. If the private owner were ecologically minded, he would be proud to be the custodian of a reasonable proportion of such areas, which add diversity and beauty to his farm and to his community.

In some instances, the assumed lack of profit in these "waste" areas has proved to be wrong, but only after most of them had been done away with. The present scramble to reflood muskrat marshes is a case in point.

There is a clear tendency in American conservation to relegate to government all necessary jobs that private landowners fail to perform. Government ownership, operation, subsidy, or regulation is now widely prevalent in forestry, range management, soil and watershed management, park and wilderness conservation, fisheries management, and migratory bird management, with more to come. Most of this growth in governmental conservation is proper and logical, some of it is inevitable. That I imply no disapproval of it is implicit in the fact that I have spent most of my life working for it. Nevertheless the question arises: What is the ultimate magnitude of the enterprise? Will the tax base carry its eventual ramifications? At what point will governmental conservation, like the mastodon, become handicapped by its own dimensions? The answer, if there is any, seems to be in a land ethic, or some other force which assigns more obligation to the private landowner.

Industrial landowners and users, especially lumbermen and stockmen, are inclined to wail long and loudly about the extension of government ownership and regulation to land, but (with notable exceptions) they show little disposition to develop the only visible alternative: the voluntary practice of conservation on their own lands.

When the private landowner is asked to perform some unprofitable act for the good of the community, he today assents only with outstretched palm. If the act costs him cash this is fair and proper, but when it costs only forethought, open-mindedness, or time, the issue is at least debatable. The overwhelming growth of land-use subsidies in recent years must be ascribed, in large part, to the government's own agencies for conservation education: the land bureaus, the agricultural colleges, and the extension services. As far as I can detect, no ethical obligation toward land is taught in these institutions.

To sum up: a system of conservation based solely on economic self-interest is hopelessly lopsided. It tends to ignore, and thus eventually to eliminate, many elements in the land community that lack commercial value, but that are (as far as we know) essential to its healthy functioning. It assumes, falsely, I think, that the economic parts of the biotic clock will function without the uneconomic parts. It tends to relegate to government many functions eventually too large, too complex, or too widely dispersed to be performed by government.

An ethical obligation on the part of the private owner is the only visible remedy for these situations.

The Land Pyramid

An ethic to supplement and guide the economic relation to land presupposes the existence of some mental image of land as a biotic mechanism. We can be ethical only in relation to something we can see, feel, understand, love, or otherwise have faith in.

The image commonly employed in conservation education is "the balance of nature." For reasons too lengthy to detail here, this figure of speech fails to describe accurately what little we know about the land mechanism. A much truer image is the one employed in ecology: the biotic pyramid. I shall first sketch the pyramid as a symbol of land, and later develop some of its implications in terms of land-use.

Plants absorb energy from the sun. This energy flows through a circuit called the biota, which may be represented by a pyramid consisting of layers. The bottom layer is the soil. A plant layer rests on the soil, an insect layer on the plants, a bird and rodent layer on the insects, and so on up through various animal groups to the apex layer, which consists of the larger carnivores.

The species of a layer are alike not in where they came from, or in what they look like, but rather in what they eat. Each successive layer depends on those below it for food and often for other services, and each in turn furnishes food and services to those above. Proceeding upward, each successive layer decreases in numerical abundance. Thus, for every carnivore there are hundreds of his prey, thousands of their prey, millions of insects, uncountable plants. The pyramidal form of the system reflects this numerical progression from apex to base. Man shares an intermediate layer with the bears, raccoons, and squirrels which eat both meat and vegetables.

The lines of dependency for food and other services are called food chains. Thus soil-oak-deer-Indian is a chain that has now been largely converted to soil-corn-cow-farmer. Each species, including ourselves, is a link in many chains. The deer eats a hundred plants other than oak, and the cow a hundred plants other than corn. Both, then, are links in a hundred chains. The pyramid is a tangle of chains so complex as to seem disorderly, yet the stability of the system proves it to be a highly organized structure. Its functioning depends on the co-operation and competition of its diverse parts.

In the beginning, the pyramid of life was low and squat; the food chains short and simple. Evolution has added layer after layer, link after link. Man is one of thousands of accretions to the height and complexity of the pyramid. Science has given us many doubts, but it has given us at least one certainty: the trend of evolution is to elaborate and diversify the biota.

Land, then, is not merely soil; it is a fountain of energy flowing through a circuit of soils, plants, and animals. Food chains are the living channels which conduct energy upward; death and decay return it to the soil. The circuit is not closed; some energy is dissipated in decay, some is added by absorption from the air, some is stored in soils, peats, and long-lived forests; but it is a sustained circuit, like a slowly augmented revolving fund of life. There is always a net loss by downhill wash, but this is normally small and offset by the decay of rocks. It is deposited in the ocean and, in the course of geological time, raised to form new lands and new pyramids.

The velocity and character of the upward flow of energy depend on the complex structure of the plant and animal community, much as the upward flow of sap in a tree depends on its complex cellular organization. Without this complexity, normal circulation would presumably not occur. Structure means the characteristic numbers, as well as the characteristic kinds and functions, of the component species. This interdependence between the complex structure of the land and its smooth functioning as an energy unit is one of its basic attributes.

When a change occurs in one part of the circuit, many other parts must adjust themselves to it. Change does not necessarily obstruct or divert the flow of energy; evolution is a long series of self-induced changes, the net result of which has been to elaborate the flow mechanism and to lengthen the circuit. Evolutionary changes, however, are usually slow and local. Man's invention of tools has enabled him to make changes of unprecedented violence, rapidity, and scope.

One change is in the composition of floras and faunas. The larger predators are lopped off the apex of the pyramid; food chains, for the first time in history, become shorter rather than longer. Domesticated species from other lands are substituted for wild ones, and wild ones are moved to new habitats. In this world-wide pooling of faunas and floras, some species get out of bounds as pests and diseases, others are extinguished. Such effects are seldom intended or foreseen; they represent unpredicted and often untraceable readjustments in the structure. Agricultural science is largely a race between the emergence of new pests and the emergence of new techniques for their control.

Another change touches the flow of energy through plants and animals and its return to the soil. Fertility is the ability of soil to receive, store, and release energy. Agriculture, by overdrafts on the soil, or by too radical a substitution of domestic for native species in the superstructure, may derange the channels of flow or deplete storage. Soils depleted of their storage, or of the organic matter which anchors it, wash away faster than they form. This is erosion.

Waters, like soil, are part of the energy circuit. Industry, by polluting waters or obstructing them with dams, may exclude the plants and animals necessary to keep energy in circulation.

Transportation brings about another basic change: the plants or animals grown in one region are now consumed and returned to the soil in another. Transportation taps the energy stored in rocks, and in the air, and uses it elsewhere; thus we fertilize the garden with nitrogen gleaned by the guano birds from the fishes of seas on the other side of the Equator. Thus the formerly localized and self-contained circuits are pooled on a world-wide scale.

The process of altering the pyramid for human occupation releases stored energy, and this often gives rise, during the pioneering period, to a deceptive exuberance of plant and animal life, both wild and tame. These releases of biotic capital tend to becloud or postpone the penalties of violence.

•　•　•

This thumbnail sketch of land as an energy circuit conveys three basic ideas:

1. That land is not merely soil.

2. That the native plants and animals kept the energy circuit open; others may or may not.

3. That man-made changes are of a different order than evolutionary changes, and have effects more comprehensive than is intended or foreseen.

These ideas, collectively, raise two basic issues: Can the land adjust itself to the new order? Can the desired alterations be accomplished with less violence?

Biotas seem to differ in their capacity to sustain violent conversion. Western Europe, for example, carries a far different pyramid than Caesar found there. Some large animals are lost; swampy forests have become meadows or plow-land; many new plants and animals are introduced, some of which escape as pests; the remaining natives are greatly changed in distribution and abundance. Yet the soil is still there and, with the help of imported nutrients, still fertile; the waters flow normally; the new structure seems to function and to persist. There is no visible stoppage or derangement of the circuit.

Western Europe, then, has a resistant biota. Its inner processes are tough, elastic, resistant to strain. No matter how violent the alterations, the pyramid, so far, has developed some new *modus vivendi* which preserves its habitability for man, and for most of the other natives.

Japan seems to present another instance of radical conversion without disorganization.

Most other civilized regions, and some as yet barely touched by civilization, display various stages of disorganization, varying from initial symptoms to advanced wastage. In Asia Minor and North Africa diagnosis is confused by climatic changes, which may have been either the cause or the effect of advanced wastage. In the United States the degree of disorganization varies locally; it is worst in the Southwest, the Ozarks, and parts of the South, and least in New England and the Northwest. Better land-uses may still arrest it in the less advanced regions. In parts of Mexico, South America, South Africa, and Australia a violent and accelerating wastage is in progress, but I cannot assess the prospects.

This almost world-wide display of disorganization in the land seems to be similar to disease in an animal, except that it never culminates in complete disorganization or death. The land recovers, but at some reduced level of complexity, and with a reduced carrying capacity for people, plants, and animals. Many biotas currently regarded as "lands of opportunity" are in fact already subsisting on exploitative agriculture, i.e. they have already exceeded their sustained carrying capacity. Most of South America is overpopulated in this sense.

In arid regions we attempt to offset the process of wastage by reclamation, but it is only too evident that the prospective longevity of reclamation projects is often short. In our own West, the best of them may not last a century.

The combined evidence of history and ecology seems to support one general deduction: the less violent the man-made changes, the greater the probability of successful readjustment in the pyramid. Violence, in turn, varies with human population density; a dense population requires a more violent conversion. In this respect, North America has a better chance for permanence than Europe, if she can contrive to limit her density.

This deduction runs counter to our current philosophy, which assumes that because a small increase in density enriched human life, that an indefinite increase will enrich it indefinitely. Ecology knows of no density relationship that holds for indefinitely wide limits. All gains from density are subject to a law of diminishing returns.

Whatever may be the equation for men and land, it is improbable that we as yet know all its terms. Recent discoveries in mineral and vitamin nutrition reveal unsuspected dependencies in the up-circuit: incredibly minute quantities of certain substances determine the value of soils to plants, of plants to animals. What of the down-circuit? What of the vanishing species, the preservation of which we now regard as an esthetic luxury? They helped build the soil; in what unsuspected ways may they be essential to its maintenance? Professor Weaver proposes that we use prairie flowers to reflocculate the wasting soils of the dust bowl; who knows for what purpose cranes and condors, otters and grizzlies may some day be used?

Land Health and The A-B Cleavage

A land ethic, then, reflects the existence of an ecological conscience, and this in turn reflects a conviction of individual responsibility for the health of the land. Health is the capacity of the land for self-renewal. Conservation is our effort to understand and preserve this capacity.

Conservationists are notorious for their dissensions. Superficially these seem to add up to mere confusion, but a more careful scrutiny reveals a single plane of cleavage common to many specialized fields. In each field one group (A) regards the land as soil, and its function as commodity-production; another group (B) regards the land as a biota, and its function as something broader. How much broader is admittedly in a state of doubt and confusion.

In my own field, forestry, group A is quite content to grow trees like cabbages, with cellulose as the basic forest commodity. It feels no inhibition against violence; its ideology is agronomic. Group B, on the other hand, sees forestry as fundamentally different from agronomy because it employs natural species, and manages a natural environment rather than creating an artificial one. Group B prefers natural reproduction on principle. It worries on biotic as well as economic grounds about the loss of species like chestnut, and the threatened loss of the white pines. It worries about a whole series of secondary forest functions: wildlife, recreation, watersheds, wilderness areas. To my mind, Group B feels the stirrings of an ecological conscience.

In the wildlife field, a parallel cleavage exists. For Group A the basic commodities are sport and meat; the yardsticks of production are ciphers of take in pheasants and trout. Artificial propagation is acceptable as a permanent as well as a temporary recourse—if its unit costs permit. Group B, on the other hand, worries about a whole series of biotic side-issues. What is the cost in predators of producing a game crop? Should we have further recourse to exotics? How can management restore the shrinking species, like prairie grouse, already hopeless as shootable game? How can management restore the threatened rarities, like trumpeter swan and whooping crane? Can management principles be extended to wildflowers? Here again it is clear to me that we have the same A-B cleavage as in forestry.

In the larger field of agriculture I am less competent to speak, but there seem to be somewhat parallel cleavages. Scientific agriculture was actively developing before ecology was born, hence a slower penetration of ecological concepts might be expected. Moreover the farmer, by the very nature of his techniques, must modify the biota more radically than the forester or the wildlife manager. Nevertheless, there are many discontents in agriculture which seem to add up to a new vision of "biotic farming."

Perhaps the most important of these is the new evidence that poundage or tonnage is no measure of the food-value of farm crops; the products of fertile soil may be qualitatively as well as quantitatively superior. We can bolster poundage from depleted soils by pouring on imported fertility, but we are not necessarily bolstering food-value. The possible ultimate ramifications of this idea are so immense that I must leave their exposition to abler pens.

The discontent that labels itself "organic farming," while bearing some of the earmarks of a cult, is nevertheless biotic in its direction, particularly in its insistence on the importance of soil flora and fauna.

The ecological fundamentals of agriculture are just as poorly known to the public as in other fields of land-use. For example, few educated people realize that the marvelous advances in technique made during recent decades are improvements in the pump, rather than the well. Acre for acre, they have barely sufficed to offset the sinking level of fertility.

In all of these cleavages, we see repeated the same basic paradoxes: man the conqueror *versus* man the biotic citizen; science the sharpener of his sword *versus* science the searchlight on his universe; land the slave and servant *versus* land the collective organism. Robinson's injunction to Tristram may well be applied, at this juncture, to *Homo sapiens* as a species in geological time:

Whether you will or not
You are a King, Tristram, for you are one
Of the time-tested few that leave the world,
When they are gone, not the same place it was.
Mark what you leave.

The Outlook

It is inconceivable to me that an ethical relation to land can exist without love, respect, and admiration for land, and a high regard for its value. By value, I of course mean something far broader than mere economic value; I mean value in the philosophical sense.

Perhaps the most serious obstacle impeding the evolution of a land ethic is the fact that our educational and economic system is headed away from, rather than toward, an intense consciousness of land. Your true modern is separated from the land by many middlemen, and by innumerable physical gadgets. He has no vital relation to it; to him it is the space between cities on which crops grow. Turn him loose for a day on the land, and if the spot does not happen to be a golf links or a "scenic" area, he is bored stiff. If crops could be raised by hydroponics instead of farming, it would suit him very well. Synthetic substitutes for wood, leather, wool, and other natural land products suit him better than the originals. In short, land is something he has "outgrown."

Almost equally serious as an obstacle to a land ethic is the attitude of the farmer for whom the land is still an adversary, or a taskmaster that keeps him in slavery. Theoretically, the mechanization of farming ought to cut the farmer's chains, but whether it really does is debatable.

One of the requisites for an ecological comprehension of land is an understanding of ecology, and this is by no means co-extensive with "education"; in fact, much higher education seems deliberately to avoid ecological concepts. An understanding of ecology does not necessarily originate in courses bearing ecological labels; it is quite as likely to be labeled geography, botany, agronomy, history, or economics. This is as it should be, but whatever the label, ecological training is scarce.

The case for a land ethic would appear hopeless but for the minority which is in obvious revolt against these "modern" trends.

The "key-log" which must be moved to release the evolutionary process for an ethic is simply this: quit thinking about decent land-use as solely an economic problem. Examine each question in terms of what is ethically and esthetically right, as well as what is economically expedient. A thing is right when it tends to preserve the integrity, stability, and beauty of the biotic community. It is wrong when it tends otherwise.

It of course goes without saying that economic feasibility limits the tether of what can or cannot be done for land. It always has and it always will. The fallacy the economic determinists have tied around our collective neck, and which we now need to cast off, is the belief that economics determines *all* land-use. This is simply not true. An innumerable host of actions and attitudes, comprising perhaps the bulk of all land relations, is determined by the land-users' tastes and predilections, rather than by his purse. The bulk of all land relations hinges on investments of time, forethought, skill, and faith rather than on investments of cash. As a land-user thinketh, so is he.

I have purposely presented the land ethic as a product of social evolution because nothing so important as an ethic is ever "written." Only the most superficial student of history supposes that Moses "wrote" the Decalogue; it evolved in the minds of a thinking community, and Moses wrote a tentative summary of it for a "seminar." I say tentative because evolution never stops.

The evolution of a land ethic is an intellectual as well as emotional process. Conservation is paved with good intentions which prove to be futile, or even dangerous, because they are devoid of critical understanding either of the land, or of economic land-use. I think it is a truism that as the ethical frontier advances from the individual to the community, its intellectual content increases.

The mechanism of operation is the same for any ethic: social approbation for right actions: social disapproval for wrong actions.

By and large, our present problem is one of attitudes and implements. We are remodeling the Alhambra with a steamshovel, and we are proud of our yardage. We shall hardly relinquish the shovel, which after all has many good points, but we are in need of gentler and more objective criteria for its successful use.

Projects

1.   Do societies around the world have the same attitudes toward "land" as twentieth-century Americans do? Research this topic and report your findings to your classmates. Relate your findings to Griffin's essay, "Frontier Freedoms and Space Age Cities."

2.   Read "The Causes of Pollution," by Barry Commoner and others, in *Environment* (April, 1971, Volume 13, Number 3, pages 2–19). Relate the article to Leopold's remarks.

3.   Investigate federal and state regulations governing extermination of predators. What states still offer bounties for predators?

4.   Prepare an advertisement that urges Americans to adopt a new attitude toward the land. Aim your advertisement toward a

particular audience. Select the communication channel you will use (radio, TV, newspaper, billboard, etc.). Attempt to have your ad produced in your school paper or by the school radio or TV station.

5.   Read Rachel Carson's *The Silent Spring*. Relate her findings to Leopold's essay.

Suggested Topics for Writing

1.   Leopold discusses history as "biotic interaction." Is this a valid notion or the outlandish view of an ardent conservationist? Support or refute.

2.   In discussing the land pyramid, Leopold points out that "Man shares an intermediate layer with the bears, raccoons, and squirrels which eat both meat and vegetables." Contrast man's position in the land pyramid with man's conception of himself as having dominion over all aspects of the pyramid. To what degree does this difference account for man's disruption of nature?

3.   If you, personally, are to deal ethically with the land, what aspects of your present life style must you alter?

4.   Leopold notes lack of ecological training as a serious obstacle impeding the evolution of a land ethic. Examine your own education. What courses, if any, have given you ecological training? Write a letter to your high school principal or the chairman of your community's school board, urging him to include more ecological training in the school curriculum, with preferably some specifications for such courses.

Exercises

1.   What is the land ethic that Leopold proposes? How does it relate to other American ethics? How does it relate to ideas expounded by contemporary conservationists? Leopold's essay was published more than twenty years ago. Have we, as a nation, undergone the "social evolution" necessary for development of a "land ethic" during those twenty years?

2. What are the main sources of failure in the various conservation movements that Leopold discusses? Notice the important juxtaposition of "enlightened self-interest" and "conservation." Is the present environmental movement doomed to failure?

3. Leopold asserts that "Obligations have no meaning without conscience. . . ." Do you agree?

4. In the discussion headed "Substitutes for a Land Ethic" Leopold discusses the various arguments we have advanced for saving or conserving various plant and animal life. What are these arguments? What, as far as Leopold is concerned, is wrong with this kind of reasoning? What would he substitute?

5. What is the "land pyramid"? What constitutes its various layers? Where does man fit into this system? How has the pyramid been altered? Of what significance is the pyramid to the discussion of a land ethic?

6. Define: ecology, symbosis, biota, biotic community, flora, fauna, erosion, agronomy, and reflocculate. Also consider such terms as food chains, exploitive agriculture, exotics, reclamation, predatory mammals, and raptorial birds.

7. What does Leopold mean by the A-B Cleavage? Consider carefully the third paragraph of the section titled "Land Health and the A-B Cleavage."

8. In the final section of the essay, "The Outlook," is Leopold optimistic or pessimistic? What barriers does he see to the evolution of a land ethic? Why must one evolve rather than be written?

9. What is the effect of the anecdote with which Leopold opens the essay? Is it well chosen, especially when you consider that the essay that follows is "scientific" as far as basic subject matter is concerned? Leopold concludes the essay with a literary allusion. He also includes one at the end of the section titled "Land Health and the A-B Cleavage." What do they contribute to the essay? Do they broaden its appeal?

10. Notice the kinds of examples that Leopold uses to illustrate the various points he makes throughout the essay. Has he drawn from a wide enough range of examples to make his points clear? Make a list of the kinds of examples he introduces.

11. Leopold defines several key words in the essay. How adequate are the definitions for the lay reader?

12. In two instances Leopold breaks into the essay to speak in the first person. Is this acceptable in the context of the essay? Or is it a break with the impersonal flow of the rest of the essay?

13. At the ends of several sections in the essay, Leopold provides summaries. Are these useful or unnecessary?

14. Leopold constructs his transitions very carefully. What transitional devices does he use?

6. Advertisement

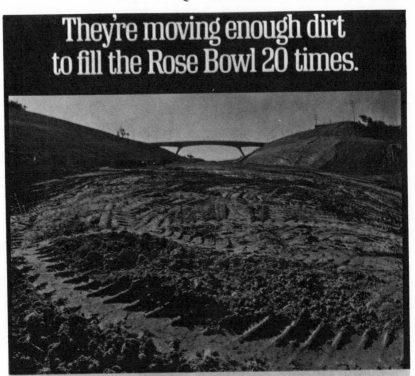

Clark Equipment Company, Buchanan, Michigan.

Exercises

Man can reshape his environment—with or without foresight.

1. Foresighted development is our responsibility, not that of the machines, for we plan the projects in which they are used! Research the process by which your state decides to build a new highway. Report your findings to the class. Discuss environmental considerations included in this process.

2. Frequently our newspapers and newscasts report issues that we must resolve as we employ our technology in reshaping the environment. Enumerate some of these issues. Discuss steps necessary to their resolution.

3. Various authors have considered the questions raised as man attempts to use with foresight the technologies he has developed. *This Little Planet,* edited by Michael Hamilton, examines conservation issues from two perspectives: the scientific and the ethical. *Design With Nature,* by Ian McHarg, stresses that, with careful planning, man can create an environment that includes modern conveniences and yet retains much of its natural charm and livability. Read one of these books—or others on related topics. In a class report, share the insights offered by the author.

7. *Los Angeles*

FLOYCE ALEXANDER

They are herding our hearts down freeways.
The architects of America say
This is how it will be in another century:
We will join with armies of geese
In the cities of weeds,
Living on grass, in love with our own dung.

Original poem.

8. Frontier Freedoms and Space Age Cities

C. W. GRIFFIN, JR.

Several years ago, in a magazine article ominously entitled "Is Your Right to Drive in Danger?" former Secretary of Commerce Luther Hodges denounced the mass-transit boosters who want frontier Americans to stop driving their motorized steeds to work and ride the stagecoach with the dudes. "Fuzzy-minded theorists" reacting to spreading traffic jams, warned Mr. Hodges, have proposed imposition of rush-hour tolls to reduce traffic volume on major urban highways and a cutback in the urban freeway-building program. Such proposals, he said, threaten "our right to come and go as we please . . . a heritage from frontier days."

Nostalgia for frontier freedoms is manifest in almost every facet of American life—from the popularity of Wild West paperbacks, screenplays, and television shows to the economic "rugged individualism" extolled by businessmen living off cost-plus government contracts. The vicarious reliving of frontier days is both psychological escape and protest against the increasing frictions and collisions accompanying urban growth.

Many public issues reveal the depth of the pioneer strain. Obscured by campus protests and civil rights battles, less dramatic struggles to retain pioneer freedoms vent the irritations of urban Americans. In 1963, the citizens of Phoenix, Arizona, repealed a "socialistic" housing code that required slum landlords to provide toilets, running water, and other decadent luxuries for tenants. Blissfully oblivious of their downstream neighbors, the citizens of frontier-fabled St. Joseph, Missouri, fought for the right to discharge raw sewage into the Missouri River. After voting down two sewage-treatment bond issues, they abandoned their struggle only after the federal government instituted court action against their city. In June 1955, against the orders of the Los Angeles County Air Pollution Control District, citizens fought to retain their forefathers' right to burn trash in backyard incinerators rather than accept the imposition of a municipal trash collection system. The exercise of this right released some 500 tons of contaminants into Los Angeles's smog-polluted atmosphere every day. But that fact meant little compared with the historic freedom to burn trash.

Even more passionate in defending frontier freedoms are the gun buffs parroting the propaganda of the National Rifle Association and others who profit from gun traffic. At the primitive level of frontier civilization, vigilantism and widespread gun ownership were perhaps a partially rational adaptation to that lawless society. But today, in the tension filled, crowded cities of modern America, resurgence of the gun mentality is a dangerous, infantile regression. Atavistic frontier outposts, such as Dallas, produce proportionately 100 to 200 times as many gun killings as civilized, gun-controlled nations such as Great Britain.

Instancing frontier freedoms in a less lethal but more visible way, the trash-littered streets of American cities immediately differentiate them from European cities. This still potent American talent for fouling the urban environment is merely a pallid vestige of the frontiersmen's talent. Everett Dick's book *The Sodhouse Frontier: 1854–1890* depicts the stark historical facts. In Wichita, Kansas, a typical frontier town, the ground at the hitching post was a stinking, fly-infested cesspool. Superimposed on this heady odor was the stench of outhouses, pigpens, and garbage tossed into the street or left at the doorstep by these pristine rugged individualists. The artfully blended aroma inspired the Wichita *Eagle*'s fastidious editor, a nineteenth-century precursor of the "fuzzy-minded theorists and wild-eyed planners" denounced by latter-day frontiersmen, to advocate controls that must have seemed socialistic: "heavy fines should be imposed on those who will throw slops, old meats, and decaying vegetable matter at their doors or on the street."

The price paid for these filthy freedoms only began with the stench. Spread by disease-bearing flies that fed on the filth of outhouses and streets, typhoid epidemics sometimes swept through entire towns. Cholera, smallpox, and diphtheria were also epidemic. Primitive frontier technology made adequate sanitation difficult, and frontier medicine was just this side of witchcraft. But the mentally muscle-bound individualism of the frontier, with its contempt for public sanitation, extorted a graver price than was necessary. Even the almost instinctively visualized picture of vigorous, ruddy-faced pioneers was largely a myth. Disembarking from trains arriving in these frontier towns, visiting Easterners were often struck by the natives' sallow complexions, a consequence of the prairie's most common disease, the ague.

Town-building in frontier America often entailed an incredibly crude combination of greed and chicanery. Federal policy encouraged the mischievous work of land speculators (as it still does in subtler ways). To qualify for purchase of a 160-acre quarter section at a bargain price, a frontier land preemptor merely had to produce a witness to swear that the land was cultivated and improved with a "habitable dwelling" twelve feet square in plan. Among the ruses used to circumvent the law was a house on wheels (the archetypal trailer), rented for $5 a day and moved from claim to claim. Another was a house erected by railroad agents at the intersection of four lots, with one corner in each of the four 160-acre plots.

Railroad towns exhibited the "impatience, the speculative greed, and the lack of taste which characterized the founders," according to planner John W. Reps. Existing towns, hoping to become important cities, fought fiercely for railroads' favor. But the railroads sometimes by-passed towns that refused to pay the required tribute and built their own. Railroad town-building was often ludicrous. Seeking access to newly opened markets west of the Mississippi, some railroad towns literally moved as track construction proceeded westward. One such town moved westward to exploit the location of Cheyenne, Wyoming, terminal depot for a rail line. According to a witness, a train arrived laden with framehouse lumber, furniture, paling, old tents, and other paraphernalia. A train guard called out, "Gentlemen, here's Julesburg."

In a letter dated March 13, 1878, preserved by the State Historical Society of Colorado, a commentator on the impending move of a town on the Denver and Rio Grande Railroad, wrote: "Soon Garland will be a thing of the past, and only battered oyster cans, cast-off clothing, old shoes, and debris generally will mark the site of where once stood a flourishing city, with its hotels, its stores, its theater comique."

Even under the normal conditions of frontier town development, the transience of population worked against the cultivation of the civic spirit that inspires the stable populations of old European cities to preserve and enhance the beauty and amenity of their urban environment. Migration became a way of life for many Midwesterners. In his essay *The Significance of the Frontier in American History,* historian Frederick Jackson Turner tells of hundreds of men, less than fifty years old, who had resettled five or six times.

Capitalists instituted a civilizing process when they bought out the original settlers of small villages. Following traders, ranchers, miners, and farmers, this last wave of settlers transformed the frontier from villages of roughhewn loghouses to towns of respectable brick structures.

But the farmers' practice of depleting the soil and moving on to exhaust new virgin tracts of prairie land nourished the frontier attitude of anarchic, antisocial individualism. With El Dorado always beckoning from beyond the western horizon, the migrant frontiersmen cared little for their present surroundings. Their attitude survives in today's mobile Americans who have learned well their forefathers' lesson to value private goods higher than public goods.

What little justification was retained by the frontier ethic disappeared with the advent of the Industrial Revolution and the accelerated growth of American cities. The U.S. was not alone in creating hellish urban landscapes. The Coketowns of Dickens's day, with their soot-blackened buildings, crowded tenements, smoke-poisoned air, and foul, gray rivers, were models for their American counterparts. But America's frontier ethic, reinforcing the warped, utilitarian philosophy of the new industrialists, produced more uniformly desolate cities than those in Europe. The older European cities generally had a form and a tradition that resisted the depredations of the capitalists. But nineteenth-century Americans lacked the architectural splendors of Venice's Piazza San Marco or London's magnificent system of parks to inspire and educate them. They had no tradition of city planning or land-use control. And they were burdened with a city-hating intellectual history expressed most violently by Thomas Jefferson: "The mobs of great cities add just so much to the support of pure government as sores do to the strength of the human body."

Flaunting the national contempt for urban values, we designed our cities as sensitively as barnyards. Riverfronts were sacrificed to factories, warehouses, and wharves, with no concession to the citizens' need for recreational park sites. Sprawling railroad yards blighted vast areas adjacent to the central business districts. Soot-belching engines chugged through the densest urban districts, in contrast to the European example of banning railroads from the urban core. In New York's most thickly settled slums, people were packed into six-story tenements at insect-scale densities unequaled in the Western world.

Yet, despite the tedious horror of these bleak monuments to greed, urban growth continued for decades without major breakdowns. White immigrants, sustained by the American dream, accepted their start in the urban slums. Successful urbanites, retreating before the advancing immigrants throughout most of our history, deserted the Commons in Boston, the Independence Hall area in Philadelphia, and Astor Place in New York. In Henry James's novel *Washington Square* (published in 1881), a character described the strategy: "At the end of three or four years we'll move. That's the way to live in New York. . . . Then you always get the last thing." Fueled by the immigrants' hope of upward economic mobility and the middle class's hope of outward physical mobility, the industrializing-urbanizing process kept going, despite the increasing frictions of accelerated growth.

Today, however, as hostility supplants hope in the central city ghettos, the old urbanizing mechanism threatens to break down. The earlier Italian, German, Irish, and Jewish newcomers never had to contend with the race prejudice that helps keep Negro migrants trapped in the ghettos. Like the earlier immigrants, urban Negroes occupy the lowest rung of the ladder to success. But for them the higher rungs have been sawed off, and the old American dream inspired by hope has yielded to escapist delusions inspired by dope.

Prosperous Americans' dreams of continual escape, if not

shattered, are fading. Slums, with their accompanying crime and other social ills, are spreading outward through the old suburbs and even into newer ones, continuing the historic trend. Current housing policies offer no hope of eliminating the slum racket. It remains the last pure vestige of primitive nineteenth-century capitalism, subsidized by ludicrously generous federal depreciation formulas, archaic local tax-assessing policies, and slumlord-favoring condemnation pricing procedures. So long as they are profitable (and possibly even after they aren't), slums will endure. Unlike the more civilized European nations that have eradicated slums, the United States has no national commitment to do so.

The white retreat from the spreading blight, through suburbia and exurbia, can't continue indefinitely. The rising costs of land and public services and the ordeal of intra-urban transportation are curtailing the sprawling development that has spread recklessly over the countryside throughout the past two decades. The carving of white commuters' freeways through black neighborhoods is meeting stronger resistance. Decaying central cities, spreading traffic jams, smog, polluted water, and vanishing recreational space have become the norm. Intensive planning and control on a regional basis, a subjugation of anarchic individual and local prerogatives to overall community interests offer the only hope of creating a decent urban environment, or even halting the deterioration of our present environment.

The idea of planning and conservation hits American traditions broadside. The successive waves of pioneers and farmers who rolled westward across the continent were as oblivious to their impact as the breakers that crash on the beach, shift the sands, and bend the coastline. Less innocent but more destructive, the industrial pirates who followed the pioneers plundered the resources and fouled the natural beauty of this continent, often to the applause of Congress. Not until the timber raiders had left trails of blackened woods and stripped hillsides, demonstrating to all but the willfully blind that our resources were not inexhaustible, did Congress reluctantly enact conservation legislation.

The most zealous nineteenth-century preachers of the frontier ethic glorified timber thieves as public benefactors persecuted by an oppressive government. In a speech delivered in 1852 to the U.S. House of Representatives, Henry Hastings Sibley, delegate from the Wisconsin Territory, denounced the federal trespass laws as "a disgrace to the country and to the nineteenth century." In ringing phrases, Delegate Sibley extolled the virtuous victims of the law:

Especially is he pursued with unrelenting severity, who has dared to break the silence of the primeval forest by the blows of the American ax. The hardy lumberman who has penetrated to the remotest wilds of the Northwest, to drag from their recesses the materials for building up towns and cities in the great valley of the Mississippi, has been particularly marked out as a victim. After enduring all the privations and subjecting himself to all the perils incident to his vocation—when he has toiled for months to add by his honest labor to the comfort of his fellow men, and to the aggregate wealth of the nation, he finds himself suddenly in the clutches of the law for trespassing on the public domain. The proceeds of his long winter's work are reft from him, and exposed to public sale for the benefit of his paternal government . . . and the object of this oppression and wrong is further harassed by vexatious law proceedings against him.

As evidence that praise for timber thieves was eminently respectable, Frederick Jackson Turner cites the lack of protest from other Congressmen and the subsequent success of Delegate Sibley. He became Minnesota's first governor, a regent of its university, president of its historical society, and a doctor of laws from Princeton University—an exquisitely polished pillar of society. Commenting, Turner concludes, "Thus many of the pioneers, following the ideal of the right of the individual to rise, subordinated the rights of the nation and posterity to the desire that the country should be "developed" and that the individual should advance with as little interference as possible. Squatter doctrines and individualism have left deep traces upon American conceptions."

Today, well over half a century since Turner wrote this passage, those "traces" remain disgracefully deep. Contemporary industrial polluters, who recklessly poison the nation's air and water, secretly agree with Delegate Sibley, but they can no longer openly defend lawbreaking without staining their image. The contemptuous, plundering spirit of nineteenth-century capitalism lives on today in industrial polluters, highway-building lobbyists, land speculators, slumlords, and investment builders. Unlike the Swedes, who have accepted city planning and public land controls for centuries, we subsidize the destruction of our urban environment. That is why our disordered, traffic-plagued metropolises are such a contrast to Stockholm's well-planned open spaces and its coordinated rapid transit system.

More than any major American city, Los Angeles illustrates the ludicrous conflict between frontier mythology and contemporary reality. The frontier mystique survives in almost pristine purity in America's Southwest. As described by the late Christopher Rand in his book *Los Angeles: The Ultimate City,* the "short-range jet set," shuttling between the southern California beaches and the Texas oil fields, lives a luxurious imitation of frontier life—camping, hunting, fishing, and ranching. Inspired by such political heroes as Governor Ronald Reagan and Arizona Senator Barry Goldwater, Los Angeles's make-believe frontiersmen still preach laissez-faire, rugged individualism, despite their city's desperate economic dependence on federal arms contracts.

More ominous for their city's future, these latter-day Babbitts cheer growth while still preaching the provincial frontier virtues that obstruct Los Angeles's orderly transition into a supermetropolis. Before the year 2000, the Los Angeles region's projected thirty-two-million population should overtake New York as the nation's largest urbanized area. Yet, the transplanted, small-town Midwesterners who have dominated Los Angeles's stream of immigrants have never really accepted their new home as a city.

Los Angeles's physical form conveys the paradox of small-town people congregating in a big city. Its sprawling unplanned development, a product of the city's extreme laissez-faire frontier tradition, has spawned a host of social ills. Unlike New York police, patrolling beats on foot, Los Angeles's officers patrol the city's sprawling precincts in radio cars, remote and alienated from its citizens. With its characteristic contempt for public services, Los Angeles long ago taxed rail transit service to death to build competing highways. Having abandoned the rail network, which could have promoted orderly development and conserved open space, the city delivered itself almost totally to the cult of the automobile, thereby encouraging sprawl. Commuters forced to drive in the frenzied traffic made Los Angeles the photochemical smog capital of the world. The lack of public transportation also aggravates the isolation of the Watts ghetto, severely limiting access to the city's widely scattered centers of employment.

Los Angeles's obsession with the private side of life is expressed in other ways. Its zoning ordinances favor the single-family house as the most morally exalted form of human habitation, isolated from corrupting contact with residential apartments or commercial development. This policy promotes a more rigorous racial segregation than could possibly be achieved in a city such as New York, with its greater mingling of land uses and its greater reliance on public facilities.

The City of the Angels has squandered countless opportunities to build public parks and preserve open space; despite the unequaled resource of twenty-five square miles of wild land within its city limits, Los Angeles has no counterpart to New York's Central Park or San Francisco's equally remarkable Golden Gate Park.

The private developers' bulldozed desecration of the Santa Monica Mountains recalls the depredations of the nineteenth-century miners, who washed away hillsides, silted streams, and ruined fertile valleys in their frantic search for gold. The conservationists' failure to preserve these mountains for public use is another reminder of Los Angeles's frontier ethos. Los Angeles land speculators pursue their frantic quest for private wealth in a desert of public poverty.

The throat-catching rhetoric of frontier freedom still stirs Americans, but at best the frontier ethic was only a partially valid response to the challenge of the wilderness. It has lasted at least a century past its time, and, viewed in retrospect, many of its values appear corrupt. Our nineteenth-century tradition of destroying our own natural environment doubtless helps anesthetize us to American atrocities against nature in Vietnam, where massive jungle defoliation and crop poisoning may inflict permanent ecological damage. And our casual slaughter of Vietnamese villagers may be a contemporary version of frontier barbarism, which viewed the annihilation of animal herds and Indians as totally just sacrifices to the white man's superior power.

Today, even in its less objectionable aspects, the anarchic individualism of the frontier is as outmoded as the prairie schooner. What has survived is not true rugged individualism, but its ugly residue—the obsession with private over public goods. To accommodate 100 million additional Americans destined to descend on our cities and suburbs over the next three decades, we must reject the insipid dream of a tamed frontier transformed into a semirural, suburban Arcadia. There is no place to hide from the stark realities of our crowded, city-centered society with its inevitable frictions, conflict, and turmoil. As pioneers on the urban frontier, can we outgrow the values of our rural ancestors and adapt to civilized urban life?

Projects

1. As a group project, do a photographic study of your college or university community, illustrating the examples of urban blight that are obviously the outgrowth of concern for the private over the public good. Document, for example,

    a. Architecturally poor additions to one of the city's fine old homes.

    b. Construction of an ugly parking lot adjacent to a well-designed and landscaped building.

    c. Badly designed and cheaply constructed rental developments.

    d. Rubbish-strewn waterways.

    e. Poorly maintained yards in otherwise attractive suburbs.

    f. Commercial development of land suitable for parkland.

    g. Junked cars and other rubbish in undeveloped areas.

    h. Plastic ticky tacky.

    i. Large signs, billboards, and other distasteful outdoor advertising.

    j. Ugly overhead electrical wiring and too-apparent light poles.

If possible, present your findings to the local governing body. Prepare and present verbal support for your photographic report. Urge legislation to overcome the problems you have discovered. Or gain permission to display your photographic essay in the student union or some often-frequented public building or place of business in your community. Prepare and print a handout to accompany the display, urging community action to overcome the problems you have isolated.

2. Research the destruction that "frontier freedoms" have wrought on crop land, timber, minerals, or water resources. Com-

pare past action with present action. Comment on the adequacy of controls now governing the use of these resources.

3. Choose, as a research topic, the history of one animal whose extinction man caused. Prepare a report documenting how "frontier freedoms" led to extinction.

4. Investigate the relationship between depreciation formulas, tax-assessing policies, condemnation pricing procedures, and the creation and perpetration of slums. Write a paper suggesting legislation to overcome the problems you discover.

Exercises

1. Consider the tone of Griffin's essay. How has he created that tone?

2. Select several metaphors from the essay. What is the effect of their use?

3. In your own words, state the thesis of Griffin's essay. List the evidence with which he supports his thesis. How convincing is the essay?

4. Do you agree with Griffin that Americans are obsessed with concern for the private over the public good? If so, what steps can we take to moderate that obsession? Which can be legislated? Which must be private and individual?

5. How can we meet the need for intensive planning on a regional basis and yet retain some individual and local prerogatives?

6. Relate Griffin's remarks about the "insipid dream of a tamed frontier transformed into a semirural, suburban Arcadia" to Philip Johnson's comments on ugly cities in "Why We Want Our Cities Ugly." Do the two essayists agree in their assessments of American attitudes?

9. *Suburbia*

J. PAUL EATON

J. Paul Eaton.

10. Regulating the Tempo and Sequence of Growth by Subdivision and Street Controls: The Rural-Urban Fringe

CHARLES M. HAAR

The postwar building boom has swept into the undeveloped land surrounding the larger cities. The low annual rate of residential construction during the thirties and the war years has given way in the past decade—thanks to the high level of economic prosperity and increased marriage and birth rates—to an unprecedented expansion in home building in the metropolitan areas. Within these areas, the highest rate of growth has occurred at the periphery. In an irregular series of leaps and bounds, farms, private estates, and vacant tracts of land on the outskirts of population clusters were absorbed into the surging city. The 1950 Census showed that while the central cities gained 5.7 million (13 per cent) over the preceding decade, the outlying suburbs increased by 9 million (35 per cent). And this is a continuing trend: virtually the whole growth in the nation's population between 1950 and 1955 was accounted for by an expansion in the metropolitan areas, other areas showing an increase of only 300,000 (0.05 per cent); central cities gained a further 2 mil-

Haar, *Land-Use Planning: a casebook on the use, misuse, and re-use of urban land,* second edition, 1971. Reprinted by permission of Little, Brown and Company, Boston, Massachusetts.

lion (less than 4 per cent), while their suburbs added 9.6 million (nearly 28 per cent) to their numbers.[1]

Subdivisions are entered into for profit. They occur where the growth of population, or some other indicium of land demand, indicates a sufficiently profitable market. Sometimes they are carried out by the original owners of the land, more frequently by professionals engaged in the business of real estate development. More is involved than a bargain between vendor and purchaser. For subdividers are dealing in the permanent assets of the community. The subdivider does not merely sell land; in all but the smallest developments, he has to lay out roads and provide access to the lots. And in so doing he is determining the main outlines and character of the community. Thus the street system and the arrangement of lots of the growing cities are in effect planned, designed, and constructed piecemeal by a number of private real estate developers. Often these independent operations are poorly designed, uncoordinated both with each other and with the layout of the central city, and totally inadequate to cope with the consequent load of automobile and truck traffic.

Farsighted developers were and are aware of these dangers. But many subdivisions are constructed without regard to the convenience or well-being of the resulting community,[2] and in course of

---

[1] N.Y. Times, Dec. 28, 1955, p. 25, col. 5.

[2] The late Alva Johnston described a somewhat exotic incident in the building boom of the twenties as follows:

"Addison and Wilson Mizner built the broadest highway in the world during the Florida boom of the early twenties. This was El Camino Real, or the King's Highway, which led to the Mizner principality of Boca Raton, the most snobbish of all the Florida real-estate subdivisions. El Camino Real was two hundred and nineteen feet wide and had twenty traffic lanes, or enough to deliver several hundred thousand people a day to the most exclusive spot on earth. . . .

". . . But the chief defect of the commodious thoroughfare was its length. While it was the widest road in the world, it was also the shortest. The great boulevard ran . . . a distance of slightly less than half a mile. Also, whereas El Camino Real was twenty lanes wide on the east side of the Dixie Highway, it was hardly two lanes wide on the west. All the world-beating effects disappeared on the west side, El Camino Real becoming a mere trail in the sand. Two cars could barely pass without becoming entangled in the branches of the scrub pines on either side. In boom maps and blueprints, El Camino Real rolled its twenty traffic lanes past a series of colossal nonexistent cities. In real life, it died away in brambles and swamps.

"El Camino Real was not of much use as an artery of traffic, but it had a vast power of suggestion. The two million lot-buyers in Florida were all seeking clues to the subdivision that had the most sensational future. El Camino Real was a startling

time sink inevitably into the status of a slum; the bad location of new subdivisions "where street systems and housing were not conformed to topography" is listed as the "first slum-inducing factor."[3]

---

piece of evidence. Just as a scientist can reconstruct dinosaurs from one giant fragment of bone, so the Florida sucker was able to forecast the tremendous future of Boca Raton from the giant fragment of road. . . . As investors studied the implications of El Camino Real, the corner lots in Boca Raton jumped in value from a few hundred dollars to a hundred thousand dollars. When enthusiasm was running wild, Wilson Mizner offered fifty thousand dollars for a choice Boca Raton lot owned by Lytle Hull, the well-known society man. Hull was insulted. He wouldn't talk to Wilson for two weeks. He hung on to the lot until after the Florida bubble had exploded, and then found that it was worth about two hundred dollars by the new scale of prices. . . .

"The bewildering final stage of the boom was dominated by what was known in Florida as 'vision'—a gift that enabled an observer to mistake spots before the eyes for magnificent cities. . . . The greatest disgrace that could befall a man in Florida was to be suspected of not being a man of vision. You were in danger of having your vision doubted if you failed to see a coming Babylon or Baghdad in any body of land or water that was being cut up into building lots. You qualified as a man of vision the moment you saw the Manhattan skyline rising out of an alligator swamp. The realtor's standard question for testing a man's vision was 'Can you imagine a city *not* being here?' . . .

"The price paid by the Mizners was soon eclipsed by bigger and bigger prices for Flagler Street property. One lot was reported priced at seventy thousand dollars a front foot—a figure unheard of in New York or in any world capital. Prices were running wild all over Miami. It was said that one speculator figured out that he would have to build a two-hundred-story building to earn a decent return on the fabulous sum he had paid for a Miami lot. . . .

"Miami was swamped with buyers and sellers. Shoppers were prevented from entering stores by mobs of men and women with maps, blueprints, and contracts, and the Miami authorities had to break up the congestion by forbidding the completion of real-estate deals on the sidewalks. . . . Rex Beach told of lawyers working all night long and drinking gallons of black coffee in an effort to keep up with their real-estate business. . . .

"The paid-by-the-hour orator, a familiar figure in earlier booms in California and the Middle West, was employed on an unprecedented scale in 1925. Experienced hell-fire preachers were found to be among the best sales-talk artists, and the Bible Belt was combed for them. . . . Passengers arriving at Miami by ship were met by small boats with bands playing, real-estate banners flying, and orators screaming. Skywriters scribbled real-estate slogans overhead. Elephants, acting as sandwich men, with real-estate billboards dangling from their sides, hauled the baggage of steamship passengers along the piers. Red-liveried buglers, standing on top of buses, blew till their eyes stuck out, and then brazen-throated lecturers jumped up and started to rave about a new metropolis or projected archipelago. . . . The greatest of all the lecturers was William Jennings Bryan, three-time Democratic candidate for President of the United States. Coral Gables hired him to turn loose his blazing rhetoric from a raft in the Venetian Pool, after which salesmen went to work on the crowds in the bleachers." *The Legendary Mizners* 235, 238, 242, 272, 274, 276–277 (1953).

[3] Ford, Slums and Housing 444 (1936).

How does the law view this problem of regulating the pattern of urban expansion? The New Jersey court summed up as follows: "We are surrounded with the problems of planless growth. The baneful consequences of haphazard development are everywhere apparent. There are evils affecting the health, safety and prosperity of our citizens that are well-nigh insurmountable because of the prohibitive corrective cost. To challenge the power to give proper direction to community growth and development . . . is to deny the vitality of a principle that has brought men together in organized society for their mutual advantage."[4] Small wonder then that all states (except green-hilled Vermont) have enacted legislation regulating the subdivisions of land for purposes of sale and development. A priori one would conclude that physical planning makes its greatest advances where land is vacant, and the forces of investment and vested interest are absent.[5] And the range and intensity of subdivision control and direction found in American legislation do not belie this assumption.

How shall this transition of acreage into new urban uses be effected so as to assure desirable results? Again the lawyer's role becomes more complex: land use involves far more than physical control. For better or worse the lawyer has become involved in the making and remaking of the social environment, and to this end the findings of economists, sociologists, and psychologists must be incorporated into the traditional framework of legislation and judicial opinion.[6] The social problems of today differ from those envisaged in the debates of Hamilton and Jefferson, and in many fields their treatment must depend primarily on legal regulation and definition.[7]

---

[4] Mansfield and Swett, Inc. v. Town of West Orange, 120 N.J.L. 145, 150, 151, 198 Atl. 225, 229 (1938).

[5] Furthermore, that perennial Banquo of city planning controls—how accurate are the anticipatory estimates of the course of future development?—is (to some extent) eliminated in this area: development is more imminent, and the planned design is not threatened so immediately with obsolescence.

[6] See the perceptive article by Dunham, The Lawyer's Role in Developing an Area, 28 Rocky Mt. L. Rev. 453 (1956).

[7] For a tantalizing glimpse into this process, see Kalish and Sutton, A Lawyer's Role in the Construction of a New City, 24 Pa. B.A.Q. 216 (1953), 25 id. 299 (1954).

Problem

In the late twenties Ribbon Realty Company subdivided part of a large tract that it owned on the outskirts of Jefferson City into spacious lots of one acre or more. About 56 acres, in the center of the development, remained to be divided and sold when the program ended. For many years this land has been used as a truck garden.

After World War II, Mr. J. L. Ribbon, Sr., sole owner of Ribbon Realty Company stock, gave an option on the 56-acre tract to Modern Development Company. The terms were $5000 cash immediately, with the purchase price to be an additional $90,000, "but if the aforesaid Modern should fail to design a subdivision plat which conforms to the Master Plan of Jefferson City, or fails to obtain tentative approval of the City Plan Commission to subdivide, the option shall terminate and $4500 shall be refunded by the Ribbon Realty Company."

Modern began working on a design which would ultimately include 145 lots 75 feet by 150 feet, with 50-foot curved streets. Meanwhile Mr. Ribbon died, and his son, J. L. Ribbon, Jr., inherited control. The son regretted that the option contract had been made, particularly when he saw sketches of Modern's plat, which it was calling "Merion Grove." He considered it "a great waste of father's land," and commented, "Heaven help the mailman." He then had a plat drawn up, dubbed it "Rus in Urbe" (see Figure 1), made some quick calculations, and submitted it to the City Plan Commission for tentative approval. The Commission was rather surprised to receive it, as Modern's engineer and architect had contacted the members informally regarding interpretations of the subdivision regulations. The Plan Commission summarily rejected Mr. Ribbon's plat design, though his engineer had assured him that it met all of the regulations. Mr. Ribbon was disappointed, for, recognizing that he was up against avant-garde competition, he had gone to considerable pains with the plat design, had instructed his engineer to utilize superblocks, and had racked his brain to find the name "Rus in Urbe."

Mr. Ribbon then filed a petition for mandamus to compel the Plan Commission to approve his design, and in the meantime sought the aid of the City Council. The latter was sympathetic to his plea that Rus in Urbe, by providing homes for about 300 more families than the Merion Grove plan, would thereby relieve the housing

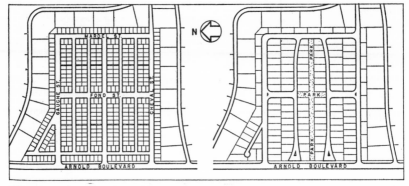

Fig. 1. *Plot plan by Ribbon Realty Co.*

Fig. 2. *Plot plan by Modern Development Co.*

shortage for many families of modest incomes, particularly veterans; that rectangular streets and utility lines are maintained more easily than curved ones, and conform to the existing rectangular pattern characteristic of Jefferson City's growth. The councilmen felt, furthermore, that Ribbon Realty was a reliable local firm, which had proved its integrity in Jefferson City subdivision work for several decades, using local union labor, and that it knew how to cooperate with the city's engineering and water departments. In a burst of enthusiasm, Mr. Ribbon offered to dedicate Gauche, Cheval, Mardel, and Fond streets to the city immediately, though promising to improve them if his plan were accepted.

The Council resolved to accept the gift, noting that the Plan Commission had not yet adopted a master plan for the area around the disputed tract. The Council referred a proposed ordinance (No. 3001), accepting the streets, to the Commission. The Commission, however, rejected it. The Council enacted the ordinance over the disapproval of the Commission by a unanimous vote. Mr. Ribbon executed a quitclaim deed, describing the streets by metes and bounds. He then applied for a reconsideration of his plat by the Plan Commission, armed with the new ordinance No. 3001 and his impending suit against the Commission. Tentative approval was again summarily denied.

Modern then presented its completed design for the Merion Grove plat (Figure 2), to the Plan Commission, and received tentative approval. However, Modern was convinced that the City Council's action in accepting Mr. Ribbon's street system precluded Modern from exercising the option. Its president therefore went to the City Council to request it to revoke its acceptance of the Rus in Urbe rectangular street system, and to repeal ordinance No. 3001. He argued that his company had an excellent reputation for subdivision work in other cities, even though this was its first Jefferson City venture, that rectangular blocks were "old hat," and that the city should not try to relieve its housing shortage all at once, especially not at the cost of "more of those Ribbon Realty cracker box subdivisions." The Council refused. Modern then sought mandamus to compel the City Council to repeal the ordinance, on the grounds that it was arbitrary, prevented Modern from exercising its option, and was thereby a taking of property without due process.

Mr. Ribbon's suit against the Plan Commission and Modern's suit against the City Council were joined, and set for trial. How should each of the four parties argue?

Projects

1.   Study the sales campaign of a local land developer. Are his promotional techniques similar in any ways to those described by Alva Johnson?

2.   With two or three other members of your class, research further the ways in which the real estate developer shapes the community environment. Present a panel discussion of the topic.

Exercises

1.   Although this selection describes a dispute between two development companies, it introduces issues that affect the community as a whole. What are they?

2.   Study the Plot Plans presented by Ribbon Realty Company and by Modern Development Company. Which aspects of each design seem most appealing? Which plan would add the more desirable suburb to the city? Why?

11. *from* *Battle New York:*
Mural of the Metropolis

EARL CONRAD

XXII

As an air wave that cannot be seen, one great process moved
through the lives of the people, the movement out, or up, to something better: it was in the street talk, in the parlor conversation,
and above all, in the constant thought of millions: it was in the
meaning of their work, in what they lived for or toward, it was
the essence of their survival and an integument of their dream: the
movement out, away from the city cells, away from all the assaults
on the senses—I tell you if you settle there you'll add twenty years
to your life, and Caleb, hearing the snaffle of talk as he passed
someone in the street, wondered where it was they meant, California, Arizona or Miami, or the mountains.

The migrants came in, Puerto Ricans from the islands and blacks
from the South, and young aspirants for the big city's honors, coming from each small town in the country, and as they pushed in-

From a free verse poem *Battle New York: Mural of the Metropolis,* published by the
West-Lewis Publishing Company, P. O. Box 1750, San Francisco, California 94101.
© 1969 by Earl Conrad.

ward, and occupied the rooms in the seventies and eighties that others vacated, there was this steady ecological drive out to Long Island or Westchester, or beyond the metropolitan zone.

And it was proved too, the landlords proved the crush, because they built a cordon sanitaire around the boroughs. The cordon sanitaire was the high rent belt, and the jam in the city couldn't break through that belt, and didn't have the money to break into it: so they stayed inside the center of the sanitary cordon and pell-melled in the apartments. The tenement roared in flames, the roaches colonized, the exterminating companies merged and became bigger; and the nerves cracked, the tranquillizing drugs marched upward. Where you going to move? You're trapped, the housewives said. A hundred and fifty for three rooms, with noise of traffic outside; and on weekends the roads were hot with the traffic of a million all looking at apartments in the tree areas.

Everywhere the ethnic millions, the material universe quantized; all the diversity of matter reduced to its minorly mutated dimensions caricatured by man into vital meaning. Everywhere the skin colors, each color in and of itself no more significant than the wing of a flea from the wing of a fly, but macroscoped by the ignorance of man into megameaning, rightness and finality. The blue eye and the green, the brown and the gray, the hazel and the maroon: all as inconsequential as the shadings of weeds but in the mind of Homo sapiens so significant: everywhere, moving in the mass bloodstream these differences and similarities: and wars being fought about them carnage over the tint on a palette: bloodshed on the hue of a nose, frenzy over the shading. There it goes, muted through the streets, nothingness vested with complete universal meaning: one color mightier than the other: fantasy equalled by paradox measuring up to abnormality transmuted into living code.

The great invisible power, the housing gods, who couldn't be seen in the clouds, but were there nevertheless, goaded and lashed at the millions, congesting, confining, asphyxiating: the big market, the great city, powerful on crushed lives, and in each apartment that little dream: Dora, can we afford twenty-five more a month rent?—I don't see how, I guess we gotta stay here another year. Besides what can you get for a hundred a month, nothing.

And the dream lingered.

Dream is a big word: it has words in it and beauty: and poets have written their dreams into Kubla Khans and Webs and Rocks, but in this, their time, the dream was such a simple, obvious material little thing that it robbed the whole idea of dreaming of any meaning whatever: a tree, a house, a half acre, a five-room apartment: and this was a dream. This was the American dream for millions: not to get a million bucks but more room.

Block by block, trench by trench, the movement inside the city went on: the people moving steadily from the center toward the outskirts, and then trying to make the big jump over the wall, into a little house just beyond the great wall of High Rent Living. If some made the jump, others, strugglers from deeper layers below, leaped into the vacated dens, caves, hovels, and they too began sharing a similar dream of better living. They could dream, and so dreaming—a dream in other times and places might have meant anything, as dreams of beauty, of cosmos-sized wonders, of magnificant humans—that dream now deteriorated into a neurotic concentration, perhaps a survival concentration, upon two or three extra rooms, and a tree. One lone tree, the sight of a hunk of grass, and some sweet air, sweet as water: this was what the dream was all about. And wherever there were couples, with a kid or two, locked in the bowels of a city block, the be-all and end-all of aspiration, the quest for happiness, was this dreaming housing thing: a plot by a tree, where it was green under the feet, and maybe if a cricket or two chirped by night.

There was no other bigger thought, or story, or dream in the city.

XXIII

It was the Bigness from which men fled. . . .

Big terror city, Big, Big, you can bet; with its Big lies and its Big truths, its Big money and its Big Welfare, the Big genius and the Big fool, the Big heart and the Big nasty indifference, the Biggety Big Big bigotry and the Big fighters and civil righters, the Big glass buildings, and the Big plumbing systems, the Big artists and the Big entertainment, the Big stadiums and the Big super super super-markets, the Big churches and the Big sinning, the Big politicians and the Big sloth, the Big promises and the Big failure, the Big newspapers and the Big magazines and the Big publishers and the Big books and the Big flops, the Big successes and the Big heart-break, the Big disappointment and the Big frustration and the Big competition, the Big bywords and the Big slogans, the very Big long highways on either side of the island and the Big accident rate, Big sirens, the Big population explosion and the Big Hudson River whitefish, Big thousands of floating condoms each morning, Big nightclubs and Big hero sandwiches, Big banging and Big birthing, the Big bosom on the babe on the Broadway billboard, the Big garment center and the Bigger stock market, the Big loss and the Big profit, the Big loudspeaker and the Big deal, the Big deceit and the Big treachery, the Big treason and the Big wickedness, the Big foolishness and the Big stink, the Big bastards and the small who would like to get Big, the Big nut and the public spectacle, the Big parade and the Big confetti shower, the Big laugh and the Big cry and the Big sentiment and the Big racket, the Big hospitals and the Big doctors, Big Big, it all is Big, so Bigger than life that it's the Big metropolis and the giant Big, the tyrant Big, the Big ghetto and the Big terrace, the Big society lady and the Big whore, the Big TV and the Big radio, the Big broadcast and the Big mediocrity, the got-to-do-it-up-Big blues, the Big words and the small thoughts, the Big meatball and the Big pizza, the Big hot dog and the Big lobster, the Big long cigarettes and the Big preserva-tive in the Big foods, the Big groceries and the Big bellies, the Big surgeons and the Big incisions, the Big law cases and the Big suits, the billion dollar Big deals, the Big bums and the Big bastards, the Big bitches and the Big beasts, the Big brains and the Big boobs, the Big body beautiful and the Big gargoyle, the Big priests and the Big rabbis and the Big ministers and the Big churches and the Big old tradition and the Big Bible in back of it, the Big biddies and the Big Top Bananas, the Biggety Big Big bamboozle and the Big sockeroo, the Big robbery and the Big mugging, the

Big killing and the Big Mafia, the Big graft and the Big You Name It, nothing small, nothing ever small, nothing ever little about little old New York, Big old Empire bigness, Big fads and Big fashions, Big trainloads in and Big trainloads out, Big airfields and Big crashes, Big clashes and Big tears and Big wounds and Big smiles and Big whatever.

Big lights at night, the Big electricity everywhere, Big families and Big affairs in the bedroom, Big thinking at the colleges, Big planning at Tammany, Big ambitions everywhere, Big climb up, Big fall down, Big handshake, Big fallout, Big partnership and Big suit, Big shakedown and Big shake it up, Big subway and Big El, Big bridge and Big honk, Big flunk, Big stick and Big rock under and Big rock over.

No room for the little this or the little that, the little guy or the little cash, the little piddle or the little tittle, but only the Big tit and the Big tat, the Big gun, the Big Park Avenue and the Big Broadway, the Big Madison and the Big Fifth, the Big crosstown and the Big uptown, the Big Wall Street and the Big Village, the Big Harlem, the Big West Side and the Big East Side, the Big rivets and the Big drills, the Big derricks and the Big hills, the Big museums and the Big galleries, the Big idioms, the Big agents and the Big sales, the Big rewards and the Big losses, the Big business and the Big ideas, the Big figures and the Big six and the Big Ten, the Big this group and the Big that group, the Big union and the Big courthouse, the Big picket line and the Big cops, the Big elephant at the zoo and the Big zoo at the park, the Big apartment house and the Big rent, the Big check and the Big tab, the Big crushing rushing Mister Big. Mister Big everywhere, nothing small, nothing at all.

Big You Name It, nothing small here, always the tremendous, the colossal, the terrestrial, the galaxial Big: Big, I tell you, so Big: Big! Big! Big! Great Big! Oh BIG, BIG Battle Manhattan, Big Battle New York, I tell you, BIG BIG BIG.

Projects

1. Study the essay, "We Can Build Space Age Cities Now" by James W. Hudson (*National Wildlife*, August–September, 1970, pages 4–9). Would the city sketched by the artist enable man to live without the "assaults" on his senses which Conrad discusses? Or are other improvements necessary if cities are to be pleasant places to live?

2. Read Theodore Berland's book, *The Fight for Quiet* (Prentice-Hall, 1970). Report to your class.

Suggested Topics for Writing

1. Conrad writes that "in this, their time, the dream was such a simple, obvious material little thing that it robbed the whole idea of dreaming of any meaning whatever." Explore the relationship between this observation and those of Philip Johnson in "Why We Want Our Cities Ugly."

2. Alan Gussow in "Where Life-Style Counts, Who Needs Nature?" describes his encounter with students who argue that "place" is insignificant. Create a dialogue between one of those students and "Caleb." Have them discuss the importance of "place" versus "life-style."

Exercises

1. Discuss Conrad's use of slang, and technical and figurative language.

2. What is the effect of repeating "big"? What purpose does capitalization serve in the final stanza of the poem?

3. What organizational pattern has the poet used in this section of the poem?

4. What devices provide coherence in this section of the poem?

5. Compare Conrad's description of the city with his description of suburbia. Which description is more complete? What is the effect of this difference?

6. Conrad introduces several definitions in his poem. Select one and discuss the means through which it is developed.

7. List words Conrad uses to describe dwellings in which the poor live. Discuss the connotative impact of each of these words.

8. Conrad points out that man flees the "bigness" of the city: "No room for the little this or the little that, the little guy or the little cash. . . ." These seem to be exactly the qualities that characterized Sopris, Colorado (see "Sopris, Colorado: Requiem for a Small Town"). Are we then destroying in Sopris exactly the kind of place Conrad's city dwellers long for? If so, how do we prevent such inconsistent development of the land?

9. If you are familiar with the big city, describe its "assaults on the senses." How many of these will a person escape as he moves from the city to a suburban home with its "two or three extra rooms" and "a tree"? (Refer to René Dubos' essay as you consider environmental effects on the physical and psychological well being of man.)

10. Should city dwellers plan not to escape from the city but instead to make the city more livable? How might the city's "assaults on the senses" be ended?

12. *Photograph*

CLIFFORD W. SCHERER

Courtesy of Clifford W. Scherer, Urbana, Illinois.

13. *Skyscape*

PETER BLAKE

Not long ago, an American housing expert, working in an "under-developed nation," suggested to his hosts that one way of reducing the cost of a new apartment project would be to string all the wiring overhead, rather than put it underground. His underdeveloped hosts were distinctly embarrassed. "You know," they said, "we've been putting our sewers and wiring and things like that underground for many years now. People just wouldn't accept having them up in the air."

In America, the most affluent nation of all, most of us do accept the cluttering up of the sky with wiring, TV aerials, roof tanks, billboards (including airborne billboards) and just about anything else that vulgarity or expediency can produce. We do so for the one reason that compels us to do so many things: it's cheaper—and what's the difference, anyway?

So the American skyline is not exactly a thing of beauty—the man-made skyline, that is: it boasts more light poles than trees; more tangled cables than branches, leaves or birds; more smog and soot than sun or stars. Where men once decorated their rooftops with gilded finials, we decorate ours with tar-papered watertanks, pipes, smoke stacks, vents, aerials, and illuminated billboards. Like children, we insist upon labeling most of our buildings, putting the name of the owner or tenant up on top in giant letters: one of the tallest, most prominently situated skyscrapers in the world, for example, is now crowned with the cryptic, mammoth words "PAN AM" (some sort of tribal chant, apparently) because the owners were persuaded by their publicity advisers that this giant badge was worth (exactly) $1 million per year in advertising! And yet we smile, a bit condescendingly, when we see the churches bearing signs that promise "JESUS SAVES" and similar good tidings.

It has been said that men are most Godlike when they create works of art, and that mankind has always exerted itself most nobly and creatively where its buildings reached toward the heavens—in domes, in spires, in campaniles. If our civilization, too, is to be known by the shapes of its upper extremities, then we will need all the saving that's available.

14. from *The Humbugs of the World*

PHINEAS T. BARNUM

No man ought to advertise in the midst of landscapes or scenery, in such a way as to destroy or injure their beauty by introducing totally incongruous and relatively vulgar associations. Too many transactions of the sort have been perpetrated in our own country. The principle on which the thing is done is, to seek out the most attractive spot possible—the wildest, the most lovely, and there, in the most staring and brazen manner to paint up advertisements of quack medicines, rum, or as the case may be, in letters of monstrous size, in the most obtrusive colors, in such a prominent place, and in such a lasting way as to destroy the beauty of the scene both thoroughly and permanently.

Any man with a beautiful wife or daughter would probably feel disagreeably, if he should find branded indelibly across her smooth white forehead, or on her snowy shoulder in blue and red letters such a phrase as this: "Try the Jigamaree Bitters!" Very much like this is the sort of advertising I am speaking of. It is not likely that I shall be charged with squeamishness on this question. I can readily enough see the selfishness and vulgarity of this particular sort of advertising, however.

From *Humbugs of the World* by Phineas T. Barnum. Singing Tree Press, 1970. Reprinted by permission of Gale Research Company.

It is outrageously selfish to destroy the pleasure of thousands, for the sake of a chance of additional gain. And it is an atrocious piece of vulgarity to flaunt the names of quack nostrums, and of the coarse stimulants of sots, among the beautiful scenes of nature. The pleasure of such places depends upon their freedom from the associations of everyday concerns and troubles and weaknesses. A lovely nook of forest scenery, or a grand rock, like a beautiful woman, depends for much of its attractiveness upon the attendant sense of freedom from whatever is low; upon a sense of purity and of romance. And it is about as nauseous to find "Bitters" or "Worm Syrup" daubed upon the landscape, as it would be upon the lady's brow.

Projects

1. Investigate the laws governing signs, billboards, and other kinds of advertisements along federal, state, and/or county roadways in your area. Or, investigate regulations governing signs and billboards within your city. After you have carefully researched these regulations, survey the degree to which they are observed. Then take action:

    a. Write a letter to the appropriate authorities, pointing out violations and urging stricter enforcement of the laws.

    b. Or, write a letter to the appropriate authorities, urging changes in the laws so as to prevent undesirable kinds of advertising.

    c. Write to a business firm that is advertising in violation of regulations. Urge the company to remove the advertisement.

2. Many companies have attempted to profit from an ecological appeal in advertising—detergent producers, electric power companies, and gasoline producers in particular. Clip these advertisements and arrange them in a collage that makes a statement about this kind of advertising.

Exercises

1. *Humbugs of the World* was published in 1866. What aspects of this paragraph identify it as a nineteenth-century work?

2.   What is the effect of comparing an advertisement "daubed on the landscape" to one written on a lady's brow?

3.   Have advertisers changed their ways in the past 100 years?

15. The Cycle

THEODORE ROETHKE

Dark water, underground,
Beneath the rock and clay,
Beneath the roots of trees,
Moved into common day,
Rose from a mossy mound
In mist that sun could seize.

The fine rain coiled in a cloud
Turned by revolving air
Far from that colder source
Where elements cohere
Dense in the central stone.
The air grew loose and loud.

Then, with diminished force,
The full rain fell straight down,
Tunnelled with lapsing sound
Under even the rock-shut ground
Under a river's source,
Under primeval stone.

16. What Is This Tree For?

DIXIE S. JACKSON

(and which use takes priority??)

17. *Why?/Why Not?*

AMERICAN INSTITUTE
OF ARCHITECTS

Why?

AIA/American Institute of Architects. Used by permission.

Why Not?

18. Why We Want Our Cities Ugly

PHILIP JOHNSON

I have read for a decade now the countless wails of protest against our urban life. The complaints are all familiar to you. All do-gooders, including myself, agree on the general horror of it all. We are righteously against air pollution, water pollution. We are against poverty, ghettos, elevated super highways. We are for planning. We are for waterfront development. We are for parks, green spaces, Greenwich-Village-type neighborhoods. In sum, we are for mother-hood and against sin.

It is safe to assume that everyone is in hand-wringing agreement. And further, we all know many of the causes of our manifold troubles: the taxation system that is tilted in favor of speculation by private persons and against public planning; the built-in confusion of our myriad local governments; the almost total paralysis of our city governments in the field of planning; the unfair Federal tax system that returns only dribbles of dollars to the city; the racial prejudice, the unfair zoning; the automobile; population explosion—what more!

But what I should like to discuss is how this great mess in our environment could possibly have happened to us. We seem to be able to do some things well. We got rich, did we not? We shall get to the moon, we can fight wars, we can make automobiles. In other words, we do pretty much whatever we want to. Why can't we live in good cities?

It can only be that we do not wish to. Why, then, do we not want good cities—beautiful cities? That is my question. What sort of values have we that we should end up in helpless ugliness? No one *wants* or *wills* ugliness. But we obviously want things compatible with ugliness more than we want beauty which is not compatible with ugliness.

Now I do not say that everybody does not want beauty. Everyone does. But everyone seems to like other things more. It is my thesis that we shall not get cities designed closer to our hearts' desire until the values of people change. Unless our *"Weltanschauung,"* the color of the particular lenses we use to view the world, the presuppositions, the beliefs, the mystique we live by change first, we shall surely go from bad to worse. If I am right, we face a dismal future. Popular faiths change slowly, slowly.

It is hard to talk about values. Even the words I use to describe others' values betray my own bias, my own *parti pris*. Yet me must try, for there are some values that help build beautiful places and some that do not. Utilitarians of the 18th-century variety, Puritans of the 17th were inimical, for instance, to glorious spending for beauty. Militarism, imperialism, royalism, patriotism, religion—whatever their other effects—are favorable for great building. So are glory, pomp, festival, nobility, ceremony, finery, magnificence. Science, knowledge, progress, cost control, rationalism, and technology are all, to say the least, neutral as to building. If I stated that they were actually inimical I would, I think, be nearer right, but in the present ambiance I dare not put myself so much in opposition to accepted ideas.

In my extreme moments I even talk against words. Words tend to become tools of knowledge, as distinct from love, and tend to need more words, tend to increase interest in the values of the description of things and not in the things themselves. Words multiply and feed on themselves. Words are for the mind, not the eye. Perhaps ours is not a poetic age. Words lend themselves to rationalization, to explainable situations, clarifiable situations, and when so employed deny us the mysterious communication by the eye, the ennoblement that comes from visions or from mere vision. Words then help the quantifiable and reinforce our preference for the quantifiable.

But these thoughts occur only at night or in despair. How can a sane man be against material progress and scientific knowledge? He cannot. I cite these contradictions mainly to sharpen the problem. How, with our present values, which have made us the most powerful civilization that history has known, are we going to proceed to the next step of transvaluing these values sufficiently to make our environment great?

The values of materialism, private enterprise, prevail today. We are the children of Adam Smith. God, glory, beauty—the intangibles in life—take second place. Classical economics emphasizes by its very nature what is quantifiable. If you can make a statistic about something, it exists. If a thing is not a number, it cannot exist. Nobility, honor, beauty have no numbers. Negro education has a number, so have calories and the consumption of gasoline. It is an interesting subnote on our attitude toward the values of the past that Falstaff's denigration of the word "honor" which could raise eyebrows in a culture like Shakespeare's where honor was a definite and achievable trait, today arouses sympathy. Falstaff, you remember, asks, "Can honor mend a broken leg? No. Honor is a word." In other words, what use is honor? So beauty, including the beauty of cities, is a word. What use is it? It does nothing for business; it costs money and money does have a use. Even a do-gooder would have to say, better to spend money for *more* housing rather than more *beautiful* housing.

"It costs money" is a terrible indictment in current terms. There is something reprehensible, something guilt-inducing about spending. Spending is respectable only if a proper return is envisaged. "It costs money to make money" is fine. "It costs money" is not.

The concept of private enterprise being more important than public enterprise is a peculiarly American version of Adam Smith. In the case of many European cities, the city owns its own land. Here, increased land values, though resulting from community undertakings—streets, sewers, parks—are considered a part of the legitimate area of private profit. Land speculation makes money, does it not? Even public expenditure must be good business. The Eisenhower road program, the largest construction program ever undertaken in history, very carefully had a measurable use: to benefit the truckers, increase travel, and sell automobiles. It paid.

In addition, roads are a milestone of materialist progress. And progress is another of our fixed ideas. It usually connotes material progress, quantitative progress: more cars, more airplanes, greater

GNP, fewer cases of VD, and what not. Progress is never ethical or aesthetic. Nobility and beauty, alas, do not progress. That the Eisenhower roads are not things of beauty (God knows) is not considered counter-progressive. "Why are they not beautiful?" we might ask. Our leaders would answer, "What has beauty to do with it? Why do you ask such a question?" Compare the funds available for highway-beautification with the funds available for highway-construction.

Business and economics are "good" words. "Business" is a serious expression in Americanese. Being "businesslike" is good. Being artistic is a little long-haired. Being long-haired is being beatnik. Being beatnik is LSD and all that. And that, as we all know, is against the law. So—applying the principle to our environment—we must run our cities on a sound business basis, which interpreted means sound business profits for the private developer and bankrupt breakdowns of all kinds for the public sector. Someone someday, I hope, will be called on to comment that it does not seem a very businesslike way to run a city. Why, for example, should private landowners on Staten Island walk off with a windfall of four billion dollars as a result of the Verrazzano bridge, while the city itself reaps none of this harvest?

As John Kenneth Galbraith has written, the only way to run a city for the people is to disregard false economies, to rise to a higher efficiency and economy and to build, no matter what the cost, a city that people will love to look at, a beautiful city. In that sentence, my friends, Mr. Galbraith (and I) have transgressed some of the finest taboos of our culture. I wonder if even Mr. Galbraith has any hopes for the future. I have none.

I confess to a sneaking sympathy for some of our "black" thinkers of a hundred years ago, with their gloomy prophecies. Henry Adams wrote, "My belief is that science is to wreck us, and that we are like monkeys monkeying with a loaded shell; we don't in the least know or care where our practically infinite energies come from or will bring us to."[1] Kierkegaard was more outspoken. He dared to call science, the sacred cow of our century, "that increasing mass of drivel."

Whether the causes are science-worship or reason-worship, a progress-worship or what, it is interesting to note that no culture in history has built fewer great public architectural masterpieces. The story of medieval Siena brilliantly outlined by my colleague, Professor Braunfels, is the exact opposite of ours. The Sienese had the

Officio del Ornato to watch over their civic beauty. Beauty was a day-to-day care.

We obviously do not care. The Sienese pattern of thought—that the city was a simulacrum of the Heavenly City—is totally foreign to our system of values.

What culture has built so little? Some of the American Indian cultures? Certainly not the Mound Builders of Ohio or the Cliff Dwellers of Arizona. Maybe the Huns or the Mongols. But were they cultures? We know many building cultures that had no writings, or at least none that has come down to us. But I know of no literate cultures which built no monuments. Two of my favorite cities come to mind—Teotihuacan in Mexico and Fatehpur Sikri in India. I cannot tell you what impelled their builders to build places of such beauty, what the wellspring of desire was in their hearts. In the one case there is no writing remaining. All who might have spoken for the culture are long since dead. Teotihuacan lasted a thousand years, but left no written records—just the beautiful causeway, the pyramids bigger than Egypt's, the majestic public scale of the civic center. Only these remain for our wonder.

Fatehpur Sikri was built with incredible speed by Akbar the Great as a palace town and was deserted 30 years later. Constructed of the finest red sandstone, it is as perfect today as in the 16th century when it was erected.

What made these people build such beauty? It could not have been alone in the mind or heart of a ruler. For one man—even Akbar —to impose an ideal on a whole people, even in a slave society, would not have been possible. No, some urge was present that we lack today.

It is illuminating to recall the history of the past 150 years of public civic building in our country. The story tells in its way the development of the *Weltanschauung* we now seem to have. The salient fact is that Adam Smith's classical economics idea did not catch on quickly and, to begin with, we built, on strange pretexts, noble and monumental buildings for less than useful purposes. I use, you note, a "bad" word for this—*monumentality*—by which I mean buildings built primarily—not solely, necessarily, but primarily—for purposes other than mere usefulness.

Thomas Jefferson, an 18th-century gentleman, considered architecture important for his young country. He and the best architects he could find built monuments whenever they could. University architecture, for example, got a start at Charlottesville, Va., and among educational institutions of its size, the University of Virginia has no successor, for all our progress and our prosperity. Jefferson's attitude was right.

Jefferson was not, of course, a New England Puritan. The Puritans were, alas, in favor of usefulness. Their faith was iconoclastic, antihedonist. By no accident were their buildings simple. Their harsh theology fitted only too well the rise of business. Max Weber's Protestant Ethic has made the connection firm. The degree to which the Puritanical streak in the American culture is responsible for our indifference to or suspicion of beauty is hard to measure but it fits all too well. Jefferson worked on the nation's capital. The city of Washington was formed and planned by monumentalists. L'Enfant's was a grand, not a practical, plan.

After such a good beginning, we start downhill. The great plan of Washington was never consummated. The Mall, which was intended as a Champs Elysées—a thoroughfare—became instead the backyard of official Washington and we have slums on the only ceremonial avenue we have left: Pennsylvania. It was only because of Daniel Burnham, a man of vision of the 90s that we managed to get the railroad tracks removed from the Mall. Practical men took over, and public buildings came under the control of the careful GSA—themost-square-feet-for-the-dollar Government Services Administration —or the nonarchitect Architect of the Capitol, who builds expensively enough, in all conscience, but even uglier buildings than GSA.

Washington's great era did not, however, end altogether with the Federal period. After the Civil War the flush of victory brought about a renewed desire for monumentality in the capital. For a time, one hundred years ago, we built on a Gargantuan scale. The State-War-Navy Building, constructed under President Grant, was the largest office building in the world and, though not great architecture, has presence and great and costly elegance of materials—materials that today we simply would not spend enough to buy. The old Pension Building, on Fifth and F Streets, built in 1885, though ordinary outside, has the greatest room—I can truly say the only *great* room— in the nation's capital, used indeed up to the time of Taft for inaugural balls. It has come on evil days. The Great Hall is now filled with desks. No more need for grand balls. Burnham's great hall, Union Station, which was finished in 1908, is now hauntingly deserted. It is a sad era for Washington. The Rayburn Building has neither great rooms nor the appearance of greatness.

And look at our memorials and war monuments! The closer we come to the present, the fewer they are. George Washington has perhaps the finest memorial of any hero in history. Even the assassinated President Garfield had the grandest, tallest structure in Cleveland for his tomb. Woodrow Wilson—surely one of the outstanding Presidents—has none. The dissension over the proposed memorial to Franklin D. Roosevelt, the perennial suggestions that we honor his memory with scholarships or trees, indicates that we have lost the sense of monumentality, or are no longer capable of the pride—vaunting, if you like—that expresses itself in monuments.

As for war memorials, we have most of all for the Civil War, fewer for the Spanish-American war, fewer still for World War I and none for World War II—except a statuary group that is a replica of a photograph. We do not live well today with memorials.

The story of Washington's monumental building is duplicated in New York. The heyday once again was the 70s, when Frederick Law Olmsted built his Central Park and his Prospect Park. Since then the city has doubled in size again and again, but parks have become vest-pocket editions. Today we simply could not afford Central Park. We can only helplessly ask: how could our forefathers?

Again, like Washington, New York came through the period of a railroad age. The great robber barons of the early century, though private citizens, had the visions of grand dukes. They built for glory. There are no entrances to any city in the world that could have vied with our Pennsylvania and Grand Central stations. In nice round figures, the Pennsylvania would cost in today's dollars 600 million. But in those days the railroads had the money and were not afraid to spend it. There was then no moral prohibition against spending. When, in 1931, the next generation's turn came for grandeur, the inhibitions of thrift and utilitarianism were beginning to be felt. Yet Rockefeller Center, though far from a gesture of profligate expenditure, like the railroad stations, made history by pulling together into architectural unity the dull, heterogeneous, conventional New York gridiron while opening it up to space, giving the visitor a sense both of splendor and of place. Again, 600 million dollars had made its mark in New York.

Today, when our generation's turn has come to build grandly in New York, what do we do? We tear down the great Pennsylvania Station gateway to the city to build a money-making facility. Then we build our little Lincoln Center, a small addition indeed to the cityscape.

Philadelphia has torn itself down, but the rebuilding consists of green-glass business blocks built by private speculation, and super highways built by insensitive highway departments. Ditto New Haven. The spirit of grandeur is not in us. Our practical age has no place for great buildings. Statistically, perhaps, we build greatly. We build so many housing units, factories, business blocks, and what-have-you. These are—oh, so obviously!—not of a cultural or public impact. There are no new great man-created spaces or monuments in these United States.

Why do we not build great cities? Why do we spend billions building roads but nothing in cities for the roads to end up in? We subsidize—pitifully enough—housing, but we do not subsidize the great amenities of the city that make housing meaningful. Planners today refer to themselves as "housers." Is nothing more important? Or are our housers despairing of ever getting more? Will there never be anything more?

And let no one ask the stupid question, "Where is the money coming from?" Seventy billion a year to defend our country comes from somewhere. Moon travel is not cheap. Our greatest authority on spending these days is certainly Secretary of Defense McNamara. He said only last February, "Building or rebuilding our cities is not a question of money. We can afford to defend our country and *at the same time* rebuild it beautifully. The question is one of the *will* of the American people."[2]

An apt (but odd) illustration of two approaches to city-rebuilding occurs in divided Berlin, the one representing businesslike practicability, the other glory and monumentality. I am sure we all know which half of Berlin we would rather live in. Yet if one half demonstrates what is sacrificed in an approach concerned only with monumentality and the interests of a tyranny, the other advertises what is missing when efficiency, mobility, and profits-as-before (or as never before) reign supreme.

In 1945 the Russians were feeling their oats. Victory was heady in Berlin. So with no regard for the functional needs of the inhabitants, they built for glory. Stalinallée was to have been a beaux arts dream. Towers, preposterously wide avenues, *rond-points,* and the rest. It never was completed and the architecture is quite ugly. And it is falling down slightly. Like a Potemkin village, only dismal slums lie behind. Yet it has a wild impressiveness. Someone (Stalin?) cared to express something with city planning, dared to make a statement. "A builder was here" one feels. The other monument of East Berlin is the great Soviet cemetery, The Garden of Remembrance, where full-grown trees were planted in the suburb of Treptow, where granite walls and marble steps were installed, where a magnificent processional unfolds in the visitor's path, where green grass is meticulously mown. As a Westerner I came away with the feeling that the Russians had suffered and that they cared to honor the sacrifices of their sons.

Turn to West Berlin. There are no grand cemeteries, there are no trees—only the small saplings in the Tiergarten. There are no *allées*, no avenues, no architecture at all. The atmosphere is hygienic. The rubble is cleared. Streets are clean. New buildings are growing up. What of urban design? What of that pride that we connect with President Kennedy's visit? Nowhere! The keynote is return to the status quo. The first job was to build roads à la Americaine, super highways with clover-leaves and underpasses, to take care of the automobiles to come. (As in America, public money for highways seems easy to get.) The most obvious feature to the visitor is the selling off of the land as usual to the developers along the same stupid streets that were there before Berlin was leveled. No new ideas, no new solutions. And needless to say, no glorious monuments to symbolize a reborn city. Nothing to mark for our eyes the horror and the glory of a beleaguered city.

Thus are the old decaying imperialist values converted to the newer technological values of the world in which we live.

Our American imperialist period of pride ended with the private competition of a couple of railroad buccaneers, the European period with the death of Stalin. When are we going to conceive a new set of values? If we don't, we may sanitize our towns, we may tear them down like Philadelphia and New Haven. We may change them to towns with super highways like the ones that keep us in New York from our waterfront and will soon cut Washington into separate spheres, strangling the Kennedy Center as they go in hopeless tangles of spaghetti. Our cities will only grow drearier. There is nothing unsanitary about Queens or The Bronx. But neither is there any glory. We can clean our air, we can clean our water. London has cleaned its air. On the continent even the industrial Ruhr river has been sterilized. The technicians can see to these things. We might even redeem our transportation system. Montreal, Toronto, San Francisco have made a beginning.

This is all possible. We shall perhaps also learn to save our old buildings, to plant little trees along the roads. But what of the city? In New York they are building what they call a civic center. It is composed of spaghetti and crowned with public buildings that are designed—camouflaged really—as imitations of commercial skyscrapers. No one has the power, the money, the authority, or—what is sadder—the passion to recharge the city. Much less the vision that Frank Lloyd Wright always preached, to build a new capital in the center of our country.

Our passions in this country seem bound up with money. They are never for a moment unreckoning of cost. The only public passion transcending that preoccupation is war. At war we leave our counting rooms and go all out.

Just as William James tried to find a moral equivalent for war, we might search for some equivalent, too—an equivalent to War, Imperialism, Religion, Glory, Pride—to enable us to build our cities, to create for our homes gardens of delight (to use Bertrand de Jouvenel's charming phrase). We have no Louis XIV. We have no Pope Julius, no Akbar the Great. We no longer have our robber barons and their type of pride. We want no Stalin. Army generals today, unlike General M. C. Meigs who designed and built the grand old Pension Building in Washington, no longer have the authority or the wish to execute heroic gestures in masonry. We can rebuild our cities, but where will the passion come from? Not from the planners, not from Congress. Everything will be cheap—cheap and, it may be hoped, clean. But cities must be great.

Nor can we look to have greatness thrust upon us. India, when the British conquered it, was given by their rulers a brand new capital city, New Delhi, which in 1911 was so great that it serves today as the capital of a vastly more populous India and will be adequate for generations to come. Alas, England is not about to conquer us. Whence then the inspiration?

This is a real need, for monumentality has its uses. Louis XIV and XV planned the Paris we know with enlargements by Napoleons I and III. But the Paris we know is a lot more useful than if it had grown functionalistically. De Jouvenel points out the usefulness—even the money-profit kind of usefulness—of the Palais Royal in Paris. But, alas, just look at Paris outside the central city! Olmstead may have been a Tammany man, most of the money for Central Park may have been drained into the pockets of politicos, but Central Park is invaluable today. The robber barons may have stolen the West, but they built our stations and they put the railroads underground. That is more than our highway commissioners do with their works. It is cheaper to elevate the highways and the public be damned. Commodore Vanderbilt was more sensitive to the public weal than our public servants are today.

Monumentality is strangely functional. Olmstead's park works even better now than when he planned it. Vanderbilt's Grand Central is still adequate after 50 years, whereas Kennedy Airport was obsolete 10 years after it was built. No monumentality. When again will someone in authority (even if it be for the wrong reasons) declare "Let us have an entry to our country that will say, as the Statue of Liberty says to the ocean liners, 'Welcome to the States'?" That could mean an airport many times greater, many times bigger than any little group we have designed. And then in 10 years the airport might still be functional. When we think where our puny practicability has put us, we can only hope for grandeur.

It has already been proven on a small scale. Example: school libraries, to serve their purpose, have to be monuments to show off learning—as Jefferson so clearly understood. But Jefferson, alas, has been followed by "modern" architecture and "modern" library standards. The reading room has disappeared, everything has been made cheap. The result: no feeling of pride in work, no relation of students to university, the relative standing of books diminished. And worse, no way to find your way around the building. Today, librarians are beginning to react, to appreciate the functional results of a more monumental approach. Monumental rooms help circulation and orientation—as well as pride. Another example: the railroad station. Compare the old Grand Central with the *new* Pennsylvania Station in New York, which is nothing but a subway terminus beneath a palace of entertainment. No comment is necessary.

Must we therefore invent monumentality to make our cities work? Patriotism, Nobility, Grandeur, Beauty, Glory are no longer any use. Perhaps we can call what needs to be done a war, like the War on Poverty. We might PR ourselves into a War on Ugliness.

Perhaps one way is to pick a great organization like General Motors and put it in charge of the cities. Tell it, "Now look, turn your aims around. You now want to build great cities, not make automobiles. As in World War II, when you served public ends so efficiently and built no pleasure cars, adapt your incredible know-how, your great management abilities to this new task. Do it efficiently and beautifully. Here is 100 billion or so for the first two years. Give us an accounting when you have used it up. We shall leave you alone until then. After that we'll see." Is this not Secretary McNamara's way with Boeing or General Dynamics? Is this not the way with the Saturn project? The Government pays the bill. We citizens go to the moon. But we do not ask General Motors to rebuild our cities. We would rather go to the moon. That is our substitute for monumentality.

The desire for monumentality might be said to be one of the primordial urges, like sex and food. Unfortunately, it is difficult to satisfy on an individual basis. It lies more or less within the power of each of us whether we shall eat or go hungry, have a mate or do without. Unfortunately, the average citizen cannot put up his own Arc de Triomphe. Yet surely we reveal our latent urge for monumentality in our addiction to status, beautiful clothes, gourmet meals, private swimming pools and other things we cannot afford, and pilgrimages to places of beauty—especially to beautiful old European cities; we pay hundreds and millions in precious foreign exchange every year to visit them. The urge for monumentality, like other urges, will, if repressed, find vent one way or another—and surely it could take a more desirable form than a devotion to ostentatious, over-sized motorcars that crowd one another off the streets. Is not going to the moon itself a status event dressed up as science? Surely the basis of it is pride, maybe pride only in beating the Russians, but pride. If only the Russians would build some beautiful cities, so we could take pride in building more beautiful ones! Or, while we are dreaming, if only it were to some great organization's interest to promote city-building, so our great Madison Avenue industry could be brought into high gear to tickle our pride. Alas, our promotional methods do not serve to stimulate society to outdo itself but serve only to impel consumers to buy bras, cosmetics, alcohol, automobiles.

Yet it is true that the urge to monumentality lurks in all of us, ready to betray itself in the unlikeliest ways. Has monumentality ever had a greater victory over functionalism than the spike-heel shoe? High heels are uncomfortable, destructive, expensive, dangerous. Functional, practical, in other words, they are not. Prideful status-seeking emotional monumentality has, in this case, beaten down common sense. In this battle I am on the side of common sense, and delighted that the spike heel is gone. On the other hand, women's fashions in which rationality and functionalism are thrown to the winds in favor of the splendid, preposterous gesture, may afford a clue to the type of pride that could be turned to making a beautiful environment.

There are signs, dimly on the horizon, that this pride can be on its way. The pride of the Bronfman family that built the Seagram Building, the pride of a town that builds a great museum of the arts, for example. And there is the monument that is by far the greatest of our sad times, the rebuilding of the capital of New York State. Governor Rockefeller, in the great tradition of Rockefeller Center, is out to outdo the monumental capital of Brazil at Brasilia, to create a modern city center for the pride of New Yorkers. This modest billion dollar beginning at Albany just might be the appetite-whetting hors d'oeuvre that could cause a moon-going type of craze for rebuilding our environment. It is sure that "practical" palliatives, "good" housing, clean slum-clearance projects will never start us off; a monumentally rebuilt capital city just might.

A final quote from Bertrand de Jouvenel's paper: "When Italy [was the richest country] in the late Middle Ages and during the Renaissance, it gave the world what is still our richest patrimony. Is it not time for her heirs to emulate her?"

Notes

1. Letter of August 1902 to his brother, Brooks Adams.

2. Personal conversation with permission to quote.

Projects

1.   As a class, prepare a brief questionnaire and arrange a telephone poll of a random sample of townspeople. Have each student poll at least five adults. Ask each adult his opinions concerning the role aesthetic considerations should play in the design of buildings to be

constructed at the taxpayer's expense. Cite a city hall, a library, and a high school as examples of buildings. Determine whether the taxpayer believes the buildings should be purely utilitarian, or should have significant aesthetic value. Combine your findings with those of your classmates. As a group, draw conclusions based on your research. Then, individually prepare an essay indicating action that you, as one concerned about the aesthetic environment of your community, might take on the basis of the survey findings.

2. As a class, attempt to devise some kind of "rating scale" to be used in judging the aesthetic value of the buildings on your campus. Discuss the difficulties arising from such an attempt. Consider the implications such difficulties have for anyone attempting to legislate "beauty."

3. Then, divide your class into several small committees. Select ten buildings in the campus area. Using your rating scale, have each group measure the "aesthetic worth" of those ten buildings. Check the construction dates of the buildings. Has "practicality" overtaken builders on your university campus? Prepare a memo, addressed to your classmates, summarizing your committees' findings. Compare the findings of the various committees. If you have not reached the same conclusions, discuss reasons for the differences.

Suggested Topics for Writing

1. Johnson charges that "Our passions in this country seem bound up with money. They are never for a moment unreckoning of cost." Defend or refute this assertion. Consider the issue on a local level so that you can examine it without resorting to generalities.

2. Outline steps by which we might "PR ourselves into an all out 'War on Ugliness.'"

3. Johnson argues, "We can do pretty much whatever we want to" and then asks, "Why can't we live in good cities?" Do you and your classmates agree on what a "good" city is? What social, economic, political, and aesthetic problems prevent us from creating "good" cities? How can these problems be overcome?

4. Henry Adams wrote, "My belief is that science is to wreck us,

and that we are like monkeys monkeying with a loaded shell; we don't in the least know or care where our practically infinite energies come from or will bring us to." Use Adams' remark as the thesis for discussion of scientifically inspired, undesirable alterations of the American environment. Or refute Adams' charge.

Exercises

1. "Why We Want Our Cities Ugly" was originally prepared as a speech. In what way does a speech differ from an essay? Cite aspects of the article that identify it as a speech, not a work prepared to be read.

2. This is a highly opinionated article. What kinds of support are offered for the opinions expressed? Philip Johnson is a well-known architect. What effect does his reputation as an architect have on your acceptance of his opinions?

3. Johnson charges Americans with several "fixed ideas" which negatively affect our environment. What are they? What effect does each have?

4. Johnson observes that we want things compatible with ugliness more than we want beauty, which is not compatible with ugliness. Does Johnson assume that "beauty" is a universal concept? Is it? Do you and your friends agree on what is beautiful, what is not? If your neighbor paints his house a brilliant purple that you find ugly, can you assume that he considers it ugly, too? To what degree does "taste" contribute to "ugliness"?

5. Of what *use* does Johnson consider beauty? Do you agree? How would the black students mentioned in Alan Gussow's essay, "Where Life-Style Counts, Who Needs Nature?", react to your discussion of the "uses" of beauty?

6. Can we legislate beauty?

7. Johnson attacks "public servants" as lacking sensitivity to the "public weal." Explain his charge.

8. Johnson asserts that our cities "must be great." Why? Do you agree?

9.   Do you agree that we all have a latent urge for monumentality? Explain.

10.   Our values have, in the past, made us a great nation. Why are they now suspect? Have they changed in the past few decades? Or have they failed to change as national needs and conditions have changed? As you discuss these questions, consider the essays by Leopold and Griffin. Do they shed additional light on Johnson's arguments?

11.   Johnson indicates that "In my extreme moments I even talk against words." Do you agree with his reasoning here? Compare his distrust of words with John Fowles' comments on words in "Weeds, Bugs, Americans." In what ways are their comments similar?

19. Where Life-Style Counts, Who Needs Nature?

ALAN GUSSOW

I have been somewhat rudely awakened to the possibility that those of us concerned with the environment are in some cases asking the wrong questions. We begin by observing that the world is changing and we proceed from there to ask, if we are morally inclined, what we can do to "correct" or direct change. If we are thrifty, we inquire what can be done to prevent waste. If we are planners, we ask what can be done to "improve" cities. If we are nature lovers, we ask how can nature be introduced into urban lives and locations; and if we are admirers of open spaces, we ask how people can be made to support population control and easements in equal doses.

Whatever their phrasing, the questions we are asking are based on the assumption that we already know in a broad general sense what should be done to make cities more liveable, and even the biological and psychological reasons why it should be done, so that the only questions which remain to be answered have to do with how this transformation is to be achieved. I would like to propose here that our view of what needs doing, while it may be ultimately correct, may not be as universally agreed upon, nor in the short run as desirable, as we have tended to assume.

"Where Life-Style Counts, Who Needs Nature?" by Alan Gussow, Vol. 1, No. 4, *Open Space Action*. Reprinted by permission of The Open Space Institute.

Some time ago, I was invited to serve as a visiting lecturer at the University of Massachusetts School of Landscape Architecture. Ten black architecture students from the Hampton Institute in Virginia were guests of the university in a two-week exchange program which saw the black students paired off with the white University of Massachusetts landscape architects to develop a plan for metropolitan Springfield. I gave a long and rambling talk which generally focused on the importance of place, and on how I felt we were products of our places. I suppose I was guilty, as we all are to some extent, of generalizing out of my own experience. I talked of what it had meant to me to grow up on Long Island when you could still roam the undeveloped fields and walk winters on the deserted sand bars of Jones Beach. I spoke of the sharp delineations of seasons in Vermont where I went to college—of April mudtime, of the endless, agonizing wait for spring. And I reminisced about light in European places—about the apricot sunsets in Rome, the sharp-edged lucidity of Athenian noons and the way the sun caressed and softened the stern temple carvings in Egypt.

If there was a thread running through my remarks, it was that people are physical, that we all live somewhere, and that the "whereness" affects us, forms our outlook, gives shape to our values. When I finished, confident that I had been heard and that the group had at least remained awake and responsive, I asked a leading question. What of all that I said did they most disagree with? Where had I really gone wrong? A black student wasted no time. "All this talk about place," he said, "about the importance of place. Man, that's not what I care about. Hell no, it's not place that counts. It's lifestyle."

The next three hours were an education for all of us. There were lots of things they didn't like, though they didn't always agree on what they were. Some of the Hampton men simply opted for change, any change, as an improvement. "As long as it's different from what they've got now, as long as it's a change, it's going to be okay," was one black student's comment. They objected to planners who were tourists, planners who passed through, observed, took photographs, made maps, made plans, but who never really shared the lives they were planning for. Some said that what was wrong with city plans was that they created middle class patterns for the lower classes to live with (though they were uncertain as to the values that could characterize a genuinely responsive "lower class" project, in contrast

to the middle class values of orderliness and neatness that characterized many present renewal programs).

There was at least one point on which the blacks agreed. They
agreed that they were indifferent to the amenities the white students
and I considered critical for the liveability, even the survival of the
city. Their environmental view was not ecological. It was social.
Open malls and parks, greenbelts and recreation areas—they found
these secondary, almost trivial. They had a priority list on which life-
style ranked higher than place. Place was important only because it
was where life happened. Aesthetics and nature were secondary.

The afternoon was a behaviorist's dream. At the same time, it
was an ecologist's nightmare. Where did it leave me and my conviction that there was a future for nature in the city of man? I had come
to Amherst a lover of open space and was now confronted by black
architects telling me open space had no significant relationship to
life-style.

Here was a confrontation which threatened my most basic as-
sumptions—that nature was necessary, that open space was essential,
that the struggle to improve the air and reduce noise was critical to
our well-being. And here was a group of bright, young black urban
architectural students saying they couldn't care less. What I saw as
the city's intrinsic problems, they were saying were certainly not even
major concerns to those who inhabited the city's least satisfying and
least aesthetic areas. And it was made very clear that to ignore the
values and attitudes of the urban blacks was to run the risk that my
solutions, and the solutions of those who felt as I did, would be ignored. This is not to suggest that others hadn't earlier come to the
same conclusions as I did. What I am suggesting, however, is that
those of us who believe in the importance of nature must ask, and
answer, a tough question: is natural open space as we perceive it truly
important in the daily lives of city residents?

When we consider the "importance" of open space, we can obviously cite first the contribution that it makes to our biological well-
being by renewing the air, cleaning the water and providing light for
the growing of plants. But isn't its greater value more sociological
than biological? With all respect to Lewis Mumford's idea of the
Garden City, it appears unlikely, at best, that we could build enough
greenery into our cities to provide adequately for biological needs
which must in the end be met by world-wide environmental planning.
I am not concluding that urban residents have any less need for clean

air and pure water. I am only emphasizing that cities must be placed in proper ecological context as a part—and only a part—of a broader picture.

Given cities as they are—an overwhelming concentration of sounds, signs and smells of human life—open space can play a unique role within the city. Open space can relieve the stress. Even the black architectural students who were indifferent to nature in the city understood the role of urban open space as *cooling-off* space. Indifference to nature as a value did not mean they were unaware of the function of open space in social terms. Indeed, the stress created in cities was not always viewed as something negative, something to be overcome. A few of the black architects—notably those who grew up in cities—described their ideal "new town" in very urban terms. What they wanted to see in planned communities, for example, was human diversity—the sight of people, lots of people, interacting not only with the place but with each other. What was sought was the indefinable pulse of city life, a cadence produced only where people congregated. One student from South Philadelphia summed up his perfect place, saying, "What I want is all the action of the slum without ugliness. It's a question of degree. Go far enough —enough people, the right momentum and a city is just fine. A little too much and you got hell. If I had may way I'd make new towns feel like a city that knew when to stop. Suburbs? That's like living in a graveyard!" By this definition, open space can help cities "know when to stop" by limiting human density. None of the foregoing, however, places any particular value on nature, as opposed to open space.

The more difficult question is whether there is a need for "nature" in the city. We know that the human organism seems to be infinitely adaptable. Yet how much noise is too much? How much crowding is too much? We also know that cities create their own microclimates—hotter and rainier than the surrounding regions. Yet people survive, or at least seem to. The issue isn't survival really; it is one of adaptability. And in the end it isn't so much a question of physical adaptability. It is primarily a question of spiritual and emotional adaptability. Natural open space—call it nature in the city— can sustain not just the human species, but more importantly, the humanness in the species. And if nature makes us more human, it more than justifies its presence in the city of man. Ian McHarg understood this clearly when he wrote:

*Perhaps in the future, analysis of those factors which contribute to
stress disease will induce inquiry into the values of privacy, shade,
silence, the positive stimulus of natural materials and the presence of
comprehensible order, indeed natural beauty. When young babies
lack fondling and mother love, they sometimes succumb to moronity
and death. The dramatic reversal of this pattern has followed simple
maternal solicitude. Is the absence of nature—its trees, water, rocks
and herbs, sun, moon, stars and changing seasons—a similar type of
deprivation? The solicitude of nature, its essence if not its image,
may be seen to be vital.*

The "mothering" by nature that McHarg refers to should not be
from an absentee mother. It is no comfort to the slum dweller to
know that the Grand Canyon cleaves Arizona. It is the immediate
neighborhood place that exerts the strongest influence on how one
feels and on what one becomes.

We *are* products of our places. In the way food nourishes our
body, our environment feeds our dreams. The houses we have lived
in, the schools we have attended—and if we are fortunate, the summer vacations, the warmth, light, mist, moods; and if we are less
fortunate, the crowding, the stench, the rats—all the places we have
experienced combine in our minds and contribute to that unique organism which is each of us. And in the end, it is not the exotic or
foreign or the occasional place that most affects us. It is the familiar,
the random observations in our ordinary life that most shape our
point of view.

So the fact remains that the major contribution of open space in
the city is not to oxygenate the air but to relieve the experiential stul-
tification of the "fixed" environment and to reduce the pressures of
the human environment. I say this in spite of the fact that the black
architectural students argued first for social interaction. In animal
studies, the more variable the animal's environment, the more alert,
flexible and able it is to cope with change. By denying our urban resident an environment varied by the presence of nature, we are reducing his capacity to cope with change.

Cities are artifacts, conceived of by the mind of man, built by
man, lived in by man. The experience of the city is in one sense in-
cestuous. The sounds and sequences of nature, however, are different.
Nature offers another kind of order—not inhuman, but most definitely non-human. And even if one were to prefer to live in the city,

the experience of another kind of order would make a contribution to alertness and flexibility. Open space offers an opportunity for confrontation—not the confrontation of a new politics but a direct look into a system of which man is only a part. Open space—natural open space—offers the setting for the discovery that all things affect each other. As we become ecologically aware, we inevitably become more humble, sensing that man is a part of nature, not versus nature, that we are indeed a part of a vast chain.

Aldo Leopold once wrote: "The problem we face is the extension of the social conscience from people to the land." When urban blacks talk of "community control," what they are trying to control is the decision-making community, not the ecological one. The notion of land as a community has little meaning for them. Confronted with the frustrations of trying to achieve a measure of autonomy over their lives, ghetto residents are attempting first to shape local school programs, to reduce hiring discrimination and to create more (and better) open housing. It is naive to assume that the urban black, burdened by enormous social and economic inequities, would place any priority on open space—on nature in the city.

Sometimes our talk of vest-pocket parks, open malls and riverfront promenades must seem like so much pie in the sky, at best pleasant, but unachievable. Yet we know that nature counts, not as an amenity, but as a vital ingredient in the mix that forms people who are healthy, capable of sustaining stress, flexible and adaptable to new situations. The urbanists say—understandably—that before we can achieve ecological solutions, we must first find solutions to the immediate problems of men. However, to wait for the advent of social nirvana while mankind's habitat is destroyed is no solution either. This is not a world which will permit us the luxury of solving our problems one at a time.

Projects

1. Investigate college students' opinions concerning the importance of nature and open space in the urban environment. Summarize your findings. Attempt to account for the differences of opinion which your investigation has revealed.

2. Read René Dubos' book, *So Human An Animal* (Scribner, 1968). Do his observations provide support for Gussow's opinions?

3.   Study Ian McHarg's book, *Design With Nature* (Garden City, N.Y., Natural History Press, 1969). Does it suggest a means of overcoming conflicting notions of how a given area should be developed?

Suggested Topics for Writing

1.   Examine the importance of "place" in your own life.

2.   Gussow's experience makes it clear that man does not always agree on what should be done with our environment. How does this disagreement affect the environmental movement? Can these conflicts be resolved? If so, how?

3.   Is nature important in the daily lives of city residents? Arrange interviews with several of your college classmates who have always lived in cities. Before the interviews, prepare specific questions to ascertain the degree to which urbanites are affected by the presence or absence of nature in the urban setting. Then, using the same questions, interview classmates from rural areas. Use your findings in discussing the importance of nature in the city dweller's life.

Exercises

1.   The question Gussow discusses is extremely important to the environmental movement. Why? Relate Gussow's remarks to Griffin's in "Frontier Freedoms and Space Age Cities." Is community planning possible when convictions are as diverse as Gussow's experience shows them to be?

2.   Gussow argues that open space serves several important functions in the urban environment. What are they?

3.   The black student asserts that ". . . it's not place that counts. It's life-style." Why? Define "life-style."

4.   Do you think the black architectural students found Gussow's arguments convincing? Why or why not? Do other essayists whose

works are included in this text agree with Gussow? List those who do.

5. What are the differences between "nature" and "open space"?

6. What is meant by "spiritual and emotional adaptation"?

20. The Expressway

J. PAUL EATON

J. Paul Eaton.

21. Roadscape

PETER BLAKE

"Oh highway . . . you express me better than I can express myself!"
When Whitman wrote these lines, they held none of the irony they
hold for us, the contemporaries of New Jersey's Route 22. The Open
Road was then the great American theme—the theme of an expand-
ing nation, opening up a marvelous, new continent.

The Open Road is still a great American theme, picked up in
our day by writers like Jack Kerouac. But today the American highway has become the prime symbol of a nation frantically running
around in circles and, in so doing, scattering debris in all directions
of the compass.

Admittedly, we still possess a few highways that express what
is best about America. But most of them are hideous scars on the
face of this nation—scars that cut across mountains and plains,
across cities and suburbs, poisoning the landscape and townscape
with festering sores along their edges. And as these highways cut
across our cities, they form massive walls that mutilate our communities by chopping them up into disconnected bits and pieces. . . .

Why have we permitted this outrage? Why do we continue to
permit it?

The reason—the *real* reason—is, of course, that Detroit needs more highways to sell more cars, and America needs Detroit to sell more steel, aluminum, rubber, and oil. If it ever became necessary to pave over the entire country to keep Detroit humming, Congress would at least consider appropriating enough money to do just that.

No force is more irresistible than a bevy of "experts" backed by a powerful lobby; and no more powerful combination exists than that of the highway expert backed by Detroit. To this Juggernaut, the ragged little band of all-the-rest-of-us is a pushover. ("All-the-rest-of-us," incidentally, includes quite a few real experts—people who have known for years how to build cities for those who live in them, rather than for cars.) Still, all-the-rest-of-us have proved to be a pushover; and it seems entirely appropriate that in Rockefeller Center, built by oil-and-gas money, the pedestrians have been forced underground, into tunnels, so as to free the land surface for more automobiles.

Part Two

OUR ACTIONS

22. *Antipolluters Doing Their Thing*

23. Seventy Miles

MALVINA REYNOLDS

What's that stinky creek
    out there,
Down behind the slum's
    back stair,
Sludgy puddle, sad and gray?
Why, man, that's
    San Francisco Bay!

Fill it there, fill it here,
Docks and tidelands disappear,
Shaky houses on the
    quakey ground,
The builder, he's
    Las Vegas bound.

"Dump the garbage in the Bay?"
City fathers say, "Okay.
When cries of anguish
    fill the air,
We'll be off on the Riviere."

Chorus:
Seventy miles of wind
        and spray,
Seventy miles of water,
Seventy miles of open bay—
It's a garbage dump.

24. We're Making a Cesspool of the Sea

GAYLORD NELSON

In the Atlantic Ocean, about 7,000 feet off the sunshine and salt-spray wonderland of Miami Beach, there is a man-made phenomenon known as the "Rose Bowl." Mockingly named for its unpleasant fragrance, the "bowl" is a large, bubbling splotch of ugly brown sprawling over those famous blue-green waves.

The "bowl" is caused by raw, untreated sewage piped into the Atlantic from the fabulous hotels and other Miami Beach facilities and from three other nearby communities. The wind and the tide have to be just right, however, to wash the wastes and debris back in from the sea and onto the beaches. And for those who can stand the stench, fishing around the "bowl" is excellent.

Ordered ten years ago by Florida's health department to treat its sewage, Miami Beach is now taking its first step—extending the discharge pipe one mile further out to sea in hopes the wastes will be picked up by the offshore Gulf Stream and carried away to the mid-Atlantic. But scientists question whether this will do any good. Dr. Durbin Tabb, marine biologist at the University of Miami, says that because of prevailing winds, extending the pipe means the sewage is just going to be blown back in-shore on somebody else's beach.

Reprinted with permission from *National Wildlife* (August–September 1970). Copyright 1970 by the Reader's Digest Assn., Inc.

With a southeast Florida megalopolis of 10 million people predicted in 20 years, Dr. Tabb and other scientists believe the "Rose Bowl" is one more ominous sign that big trouble lies ahead for that supposedly limitless resource on which the booming Florida economy is built, the sea and the beaches.

Fishermen, professional divers and marine scientists, whose lives are entwined with the sea, report similar situations all along America's coastlines.

Filter cigarette butts, bandages and bubblegum have been found in stomachs of fish caught near New York City's sewage sludge dumping ground 8 to 10 miles out in the Atlantic.

Nightmarish Beach Scenes

Some northern New Jersey beaches near the Atlantic shipping lane into New York Harbor have been turned into a nightmarish scene of tar from oil slicks, plastic bottles, broken dolls, even dead animals thrown into garbage somewhere.

People are sometimes driven from their waterfront homes in Galveston Bay in Texas near the Gulf of Mexico by the stench from thousands of decaying fish killed by pollution.

In the Panacea, Florida, area on the Gulf Coast, one of the state's last national frontiers, crab fishermen are coming in with only a tenth of their catch of five years ago, while real estate and land developers fill in and destroy hundreds of acres of fertile marsh areas, the Army Corps of Engineers is planning to cut new waterways, and industry pours poisonous wastes down once wild rivers into the Gulf.

Batches of mackerel caught in Pacific Ocean waters off central California last year contained so much DDT that they were impounded by federal health officials as unfit for human consumption, while in the sea off a southern U.S. coast, scientists have found miles-long slicks containing pesticide levels 10,000 times higher than surrounding waters.

"If only I could get the majority of Americans under the surface of the sea to witness what's going on," says Dr. Rimmon C. Fay, a collector of marine specimens who has been diving in the Pacific off Los Angeles for years. When he turns over rocks now in that undersea wasteland caused by sewage and industrial pollution, he finds, "it's foul and putrid underneath."

Throughout history we've believed that at the sea's edge man's power to destroy stopped and nature's invincibility began. In her 1951 book *The Sea Around Us,* even Rachel Carson saw the oceans as one last haven, safe forever. How could it be otherwise, when the oceans are so vast the continents are just islands in their midst, so deep a Mount Everest could be lost beneath their surface, so powerful their waves have tossed a 2,600-ton breakwater around like a cork? How does one pollute the volume of the sea, 350 million cubic miles? How poison an environment so rich it harbors 200,000 species of life?

Yet last year Stanford University ecologist Paul Ehrlich projected the end of all important life in the sea by 1979, and the probable end of the human species shortly thereafter, in a grim scenario based on current trends. I've talked to Dr. Ehrlich and other ecologists since, and there is no disagreement among them that the oceans are on the way to destruction. The only issue is when. Some scientists say that it will take perhaps 50 years at the present rate.

The vulnerability of the marine environment becomes dramatically clear when we realize that even though the oceans blanket three-fourths of the earth, their productivity is mostly limited to the rich waters over the continental shelves, narrow bands of undersea lands extending from our coastlines. Eighty per cent of the world's saltwater fish catch is taken from these shallow coastal waters that make up only a tiny fraction of the total sea area. In addition, almost 70 per cent of all usable fish and shellfish spend a crucial part of their lives in the estuaries—the coastal bays, wetlands and river mouths—that are 20 times more fertile than the open sea, seven times more productive than a wheatfield.

Cut the chain of life in the coastal marshes and bays, destroy the myriad bottom organisms and pollute the waters above the continental shelves, and inevitably we will eliminate the great ocean fisheries that are vital in feeding an exploding world population.

Pollution or overfishing, and sometimes both, have gouged fisheries around the world. Several bottom fish species off the Pacific Northwest have been virtually exhausted by Russian fleets with factory ships that take the bounty home all canned and labeled. The once-mammoth sardine fishery off California is now gone. The croaker, a popular food fish, has virtually disappeared from much of its native East Coast waters. Off New York, fish are becoming afflicted with a strange disease that rots away fins and tails, and in

dirty Pacific waters off Southern California, fish are being found
with high rates of deformities and disease.

The High Price of Progress

Today our accelerating exploitation of the marine environment in
the name of "progress" at any price is aimed directly at the continental shelf and its coastal resources, the tiny Achilles Heel of the
sea. In our greedy rush to create more land, vital United States
coastal wetlands are being dredged and filled for highways, industry, bridges, waterfront homes—to the tune of almost 900 square
miles in 20 years. In spite of scientists' warnings, this continues at
an accelerating pace from Galveston to Chesapeake Bay. Meanwhile,
our remaining estuaries are fed 30 billion gallons of sewage and industrial wastes every day, poisoning fish, choking out oyster and
clam beds, and rendering the bays and wetlands unfit for almost any
use.

While the vise tightens on the critical in-shore areas that lace
our coastlines, the pressure builds on the ocean itself. More and
more, the continental shelf waters and beyond are a tempting dumping ground for our garbage, especially for those cities and industries looking for a new way to ease the burden of the national
cleanup push on inland waters.

In 1968 alone, 37 million tons of solid wastes were dumped in
ocean waters off the United States. The wastes—taken out to sea by
barge and ship—include garbage and trash, waste oil, dredging
spoils, industrial acids, caustics, cleaners, sludges and waste liquor,
airplane parts, junked automobiles, spoiled food, and even radioac-
tive materials. During his papyrus boat trip in the Atlantic last year,
author-explorer Thor Heyerdahl sighted plastic bottles, squeeze
tubes, oil and other trash that had somehow been swept on the cur-
rents to mid-ocean.

One big new proposal calls for piping the concentrated wastes
of up to 50 industries in the Delaware River Valley more than 80
miles out to sea. But Dr. Howard Sanders of the Woods Hole Ocean-
ographic Institute in Massachusetts says wastes could wreak even
more havoc on low tolerance life in the ancient, almost unvarying
environment of the deep sea than in a little stream in our backyard.

Loose Dumping Regulations

Regulations on ocean dumping and other activities are so loose now that it amounts to every-man-for-himself on the high seas. A chief regulator, the United States Army Corps of Engineers, recently confirmed that it didn't even know how many ocean-dumping permits it has issued. And "letters of permission" handed out by the Corps for dumping more than three miles off our coasts are, the agency admits, "really an acknowledgement that anyone can do anything they please when outside our jurisdiction."

As yet, no one really knows who has what rights and responsibilities in the ocean environment, and state, federal and international jurisdictions remain in their historically chaotic tangle. The origin of national sovereignty over the first three miles of sea bed was the range of a cannon shot in the 17th Century.

Perhaps more than any other problem, the dramatic, sudden oil-well blowouts in the sea and the oil tanker breakups have begun to awaken us to the total inadequacy of our present ocean policies. The list of places where oil has blackened beaches, killed untold thousands of birds, and posed lingering threats to marine animal and plant life already includes many of the great recreational areas of this nation and the world: Florida, the Gulf Coast, New England, New Jersey, Puerto Rico, Southern California, southern England.

What famous coastline will be next? According to a report last year by the President's Panel on Oil Spills, we can expect a Santa Barbara-scale disaster every year by 1980 if present trends continue. Yet in a shocking invitation for trouble, we will be drilling 3,000 to 5,000 new undersea oil wells worldwide each year by 1980, even as the experts confirm we do not possess the technology to contain the oil from ocean disasters. And oil-carrying tankers are being built to monumental scales, cutting transportation costs but increasing the risks of gigantic spills.

How many more oil spills like the one in the Santa Barbara Channel and the break-up of *Torrey Canyon* off England will it take before all nations realize the human race is now so populous and generates so much waste that we can no longer treat the environment as if it were created for our limitless plunder?

Radioactivity from nuclear fallout can be found in any 50-gallon sample of water taken anywhere in the sea. Investigators of a massive die-off of sea birds off Britain last year found unusually high counts of toxic industrial chemicals used in making paints and plastics. Because of the use of toxic, persistent pesticides worldwide, species of sea birds such as the brown pelican have been pushed to the brink of extinction over large portions of their ranges, and there is evidence these poisons can attack phytoplankton, a food fundamental in the chain of ocean life.

Ironically, while we continue the gruesome process of polluting the sea, we are laying big new hopes on ocean space for everything from floating jetports to housing developments. The conclusion is unavoidable. If tough, intelligent action is not taken now, we will make the same wreckage of the oceans as we have of the land and of our sprawling, decaying cities. There will be more reckless exploitation, user conflicts, gigantic oil spills and other environmental disasters, and the ultimate destruction of marine life.

And the greatest losers of all will be the people of America and the world—the hundreds of millions of people to whom the coastlines and the sea mean recreation, or a home, or a livelihood, or peace and inspiration, or—because of the food provided for whole nations by the great fisheries—survival itself. Destroy this vital frontier, and in effect we will be slamming the door on our last chance for a livable world and for a decent future for generations to come.

Steps to Survival

The day is already tragically late, but there is still reason to hope. As astronaut Neil Armstrong expressed it, "We citizens of earth, who can solve the problems of leaving earth, can also solve the problems of staying on it." But make no mistake, it is going to be a tremendous task. Turning back the massive assault on the sea and meeting our other staggering environmental problems will mean dramatic modifications in our present policies and priorities, including, at the very least, the following three steps:

1. We must end, by 1975, all dumping of wastes into the sea, the Great Lakes and the coastal areas of our rivers and bays, except for liquid wastes treated at least to levels equal to the natural quality of the ocean waters.

Rather than using the sea as a last-ditch catchall for our wastes, our only rational choice now is to put our sophisticated technology to work finding ways to recycle our wastes back into the economy as useful new products. As Dr. Athelstan Spilhaus, president of the American Association for the Advancement of Science, said, "We are running out of an 'away' to throw things away."

2. We must prohibit any new activity—from building offshore jetports to the drilling of additional oil wells—until we set tough, new controls to avoid the chaos and destruction in the sea that is everywhere apparent on the land.

And for once the public must be fully informed and consulted at every step in decisions on whether cities are built off our coast, whether a new sea horizon is created with the paraphernalia of marine industry, whether huge new supertankers whose wrecks could smear whole coastlines with oil will be allowed.

We should never have permitted oil drilling anywhere under the sea until we understood and could control the dangers. Stricter enforcement of regulations for offshore oil wells is not a sufficient answer. Now, the only logical course is to halt *all* drilling in ecologically sensitive areas—such as the Santa Barbara Channel—and to prohibit new drilling *anywhere,* until there is convincing evidence it will not harm the marine environment, and until we have the technology to contain oil spills. Until we know more, all our untapped oil and mineral deposits under federal jurisdiction in the sea should be held unexploited in a National Marine Resources Trust, which should be established immediately.

3. We must halt the reckless dredging and filling of priceless wetlands and the carving up of ocean front in the name of "progress."

Faced with a coastal environment crisis, Maryland, Massachusetts and the San Francisco Bay area, among others, have taken first steps toward outlawing the "right to destroy" that has in effect been claimed by private interest lobbies, and set new standards to protect remaining wetlands.

Curtailing these long-standing practices is not easy. But the framework for these desperately needed new national standards could—and should—be taken in this session of Congress. The Marine Environment and Pollution Control Act which I introduced earlier this year would do this. Under its provisions, the Secretary of the Interior would take on major new responsibilities to protect that part of the ocean environment under his jurisdiction, at the same time setting a model which the states could well follow in their own parts of the seabed. This kind of legislation would be only a beginning in saving our oceans.

These "environmental quality" policies will be adopted only when the majority of Americans demand them in a sustained political action drive at every level of this society. There will be action in the public interest only when the land developers, the oil interests, Congress and local governments know the public means business. Citizens must take a stand now for their friend, the sea. They must use every device within the political process to see that it is protected.

Finally, all nations must together establish an International Policy on the Sea that sacrifices narrow self-interests for the protection of this vast domain that is a common heritage of all mankind. It is a challenge that will test our intelligence as a species, but a task of highest priority for the future of the human species. We must acknowledge our interdependence with all of nature, including the sea, rejecting the prevailing philosophy of Western civilization that man can dominate the planet while ignoring the works and forces of nature. For as Thoreau said: "What is the use of a house if you haven't got a tolerable planet to put it on?"

Projects

1. Research the pollution laws governing the Great Lakes, our nation's inland oceans. Present to you class an informative report summarizing laws governing pollution of the Great Lakes, particularly noting the dates on which the laws were passed and the legislative bodies agreeing to abide by the laws. Explain why these laws failed to prevent serious pollution of the lakes. What lessons can we learn from this example?

2. Investigate steps that have been taken to resolve international conflicts regarding the use of ocean resources. Narrow the topic and treat it in a documented paper.

3. Nelson believes we must find ways to recycle wastes. Research the waste recycling processes that produce useful new materials. Discuss steps that must be taken before recycling will be an economically feasible and socially accepted practice. (See "The New

Resource" by Robert R. Grinstead in *Environment,* Volume 12, Number 10, December, 1970.)

Suggested Topics for Writing

1. Nelson writes that "the human race is now so populous and generates so much waste that we can no longer treat the environment as if it were created for our limitless plunder." Has recent emphasis on environmental issues motivated sound environmental action? Consider decisions of your local governing body that have caused or prevented negative effects on the community environment. Write a paper discussing these decisions as evidence of your community's concern—or lack of it—for the environment.

2. Nelson argues that we must stop the "reckless dredging and filling of priceless wetland and the carving up of ocean front in the name of 'progress'." Define "progress." As you plan your definition, consider the difference between progress as the land developer and the conservationist might define it.

Exercises

1. Gaylord Nelson, a U. S. senator from Wisconsin, has long been active in conservation issues. Discuss his apparent knowledge of issues relating to ocean pollution. What proportion of this essay is fact, what proportion assertion?

2. Although much of the essay is factual, it is not stylistically colorless or without metaphor. Examine Nelson's diction. Characterize it.

3. What techniques has Nelson used to make facts and statistics interesting?

4. Nelson reports that Miami Beach, ordered by Florida's health department to treat its sewage, is extending its sewage discharge pipe one mile farther out to sea. Discuss this action as symbolic of much of the action that we, as a nation, have taken to "treat" our environmental ills.

5. Summarize present ocean dumping policies. Discuss means by which ocean dumping could be halted. Particularly consider measures to prevent greater pollution of the oceans as a result of the press for inland cleanup.

25. Dam Outrage: The Story of the Army Engineers

ELIZABETH B. DREW

The St. Croix River, one of the few remaining wild rivers in the nation, forms a stretch of the border between Wisconsin and Minnesota before it runs into the Mississippi below Minneapolis. Not long ago, Senator Gaylord Nelson of Wisconsin discovered that the Army Corps of Engineers was considering the construction of a hundred-foot-high dam on the St. Croix. At the same time, Nelson and Senator Walter Mondale of Minnesota were trying to win legislation that would preserve the river in its natural state. Nelson took the unusual step of going before a congressional committee to oppose a Corps project in his own state. "The Corps of Engineers," he said, "is like that marvelous little creature, the beaver, whose instinct tells him every fall to build a dam wherever he finds a trickle of water. But at least he has a purpose—to store up some food underwater and create a livable habitat for the long winter. Like the Corps, this little animal frequently builds dams he doesn't need, but at least he doesn't ask the taxpayer to foot the bill."

Few politicians publicly criticize the Corps, because almost all of them want something from it at some point—a dam, a harbor, a flood-control project. A combination of Corps diplomacy and congressional mutuality keeps most of the politicians content, and quiet. The overwhelming majority of Corps projects are attractive federal bonuses, given free of charge to communities—some local contributions may be involved in small flood-control or municipal-water-supply projects—and therefore they are highly prized. "They take care of all of the states," said one Senate aide. "If there's water in a faucet in one of them, they'll go in there and build a dam."

There is no question that the civil works program of the Army Corps of Engineers, viewed over its long history, has benefited the country. It has made waterways navigable and provided hydroelectric power and flood control. Communities to which it has brought help have been genuinely grateful. Now, however, it is a prime example of a bureaucracy that is outliving its rationale, and that is what is getting it into trouble. As the Corps, impelled by bureaucratic momentum and political accommodation, has gone about its damming and dredging and "straightening" of rivers and streams, it has brought down upon itself the wrath of more and more people disturbed about the effects on the environment. A secret poll taken by the White House last year showed environmental concerns to be second only to Vietnam in the public mind. This rather sudden general awareness of the science of ecology—the interrelationships between organisms and their environment—has brought projects which disturb the environment and the ecology, as Corps projects do, under unprecedented attack. The Corps' philosophy, on the other hand, was recently expressed in a speech by its chief, Lieutenant General F. J. Clarke. "With our country growing the way it is," he said, "we cannot simply sit back and let nature take its course."

Criticism of the Corps and what its programs are all about is not based solely on environmental issues. The broader question, given the claims on our national resources, is whether it makes sense to continue to wink at traditional public works programs, and the self-serving politics which sustain them. The nation is now committed, for example, to making Tulsa, Oklahoma, and Fort Worth, Texas, into seaports, although each is about 400 miles from the sea, at costs of at least $1.2 billion and $1 billion respectively. There are other questions that might be raised at this point, such as whether subsidizing the barge industry should be a national priority; or whether we want to continue to dredge and fill estuaries and build flood-control projects for the benefit of real estate developers and wealthy farmers. The Army Corps of Engineers and its work have been a very important force in American life, with few questions asked. Yet it is not fair simply to castigate the Corps, for the politicians have made the decisions and the public has gone along. General Clarke had a point when he said that the Corps is being put "in the unhappy and, I can't help feeling, rather unfair position of being blamed for presenting a bill by people who have forgotten that they ate the dinner."

The Corps is part of a growing hodgepodge of federal bureaucracies and programs that work at cross-purposes. The Department of Agriculture drains wetlands while the Department of Interior tries to preserve them. The Corps dams wild rivers while the Department of Interior tries to save them. The Corps and the Bureau of Reclamation in Interior provide farmlands for crops which farmers are paid not to produce. The government spent $77 million to build the Glen Elder Dam in Kansas, a Bureau of Reclamation project which provided land to produce feed grains, for which the government pays out hundreds of millions of dollars a year to retire. The Tennessee Valley Authority is also still building dams, and it does strip-mining.

But of these water programs, the Corps' is by far the largest. Each year Congress gives it more than a billion dollars, and each year's budget represents commitments to large spending in the future. In a deliberate effort to spread the money around, new projects are begun and ones already under way are permitted to take longer to complete, in the end driving up the costs of all of them.

The annual Public Works appropriations bill provides money for, among others, the Panama Canal, the Water Pollution Control Administration and the Bureau of Reclamation in the Interior Department, and various public power administrations, as well as the Corps of Engineers. This year it came to $2.5 billion, of which the Corps received $1.1 billion. The Corps is now at work on 275 projects. The total future cost of these will be $13.5 billion, not accounting for the customary price increases. Another 452 projects have been authorized by Congress, but have not yet been started. The Corps says that the total cost of these would be another $10 billion, clearly an underestimation of some magnitude. For every project to which the country is already committed, the Corps, the politicians, and the local interests who stand to gain have many, many more in mind.

The Corps' official history traces its beginnings to a colonel who dug trenches "in the darkness of the morning" during the Battle of Bunker Hill, and the subsequent orders of President Washington to establish a corps of military engineers and a school to train them. In 1802, the Corps was established, and West Point was designated to provide its members. The history of the Corps is interwoven with that of the country and its frontier ethic. It is a very proud agency. "They led the way," its history says, "in exploring the great West. They were the pathfinders sent out by a determined government at Washington. They guided, surveyed, mapped, and fought Indians and nature across the continent. . . . They made surveys for work on the early canals and railroads. They extended the National Road from Cumberland to the Ohio and beyond. They made the Ohio, Missouri, and Mississippi safe for navigation in the Middle West. They opened up harbors for steamships on the Great Lakes." After the war with Mexico, in which "the part played by the Army Engineer officers was impressive . . . the last segment of the great Western Empire was soon annexed. These things were all accomplished by the application of America's greatest power. That is the power of Engineering Character, Engineering Leadership, and Engineering Knowledge. All employed to fulfill our destiny." Following the Civil War, the civil works program of the Corps "was revived to benefit all sections of the reunited nation," and that is how the Corps has been fulfilling our destiny ever since. In 1936 the Corps was given major responsibility for flood control (until then largely a local function).

The major activities of the Corps are the damming, widening, straightening, and deepening of rivers for barge navigation, building harbors for shipping, and construction of dams and levees and reservoirs for flood control. It also works on disaster relief and tries to prevent beach erosion. A project can serve several purposes: building waterways, providing flood control, hydroelectric power, or water supply. As the Corps completed the most clearly needed projects in these categories, it found new purposes, or rationales, for its dams. The newer justifications are recreation and pollution treatment.

Pollution treatment (the government calls it "low-flow augmentation") is provided by releasing water from a dam to wash the wastes downstream. But there are now more effective and less expensive ways of dealing with pollution.

Recreation is provided in the form of still-water lakes behind the dam, for speedboating, swimming, and fishing. But the fish that were previously there often do not continue to breed in the stilled water. And the recreation, not to mention the scenery, of the natural river that used to be there, is gone. A flood-control channel is usually surrounded by cement banks, and the trees are cut down when a levee is built. When the water in a reservoir is let out during the dry months, or for "low-flow augmentation," the "recreation" area can become a mud flat.

These problems arise because the Corps of Engineers' mission has been narrowly defined. Other ways of dealing with transportation, power, and pollution are not in the Corps' jurisdiction, so the Corps is left to justifying what it is permitted to do. What hydroelectric power is left to be developed will make a very small contribution to the nation's power needs. The Corps builds its projects on sound engineering principles. If a highway cuts through a park or a city, or a dam floods more land than it protects, those are the breaks. A "straight" river is an engineer's idea of what a river ought to be. A talk with a Corps man will bring out a phrase like, "When we built the Ohio River . . ."

The Corps argues that having military men conduct civil works "is an advantage of outstanding importance to national defense." Actually, the military men in the civil works section of the Army Corps of Engineers represent only a thin superstructure over a large civilian bureaucracy. Most of the 1100-man uniformed Corps work solely on military construction. The civil works section of the Corps, in contrast, comprises about 200 military men, and under their direction, 32,000 civilians.

Generally, the career military engineers come from the top of their class at West Point, or from engineering schools. Once they join the Corps, they rotate between military and civil work, usually serving in the civil works division for three-year tours. The civil work is sought after, because it offers unusual responsibility and independence in the military system, and the experience is necessary for reaching the high ranks of the Corps. Through the civil work, a Corps officer can gain a sharpening of political acumen that is necessary for getting to the top. And there is the tradition: "The Corps built the Panama Canal," one officer said, "and every Corps man knows that Robert E. Lee worked on flood control on the Mississippi." It is a secure life, and when he retires, a military corps officer can get a good job with a large engineering firm or become director of a port authority.

The civilian bureaucracy is something else. The Corps, like other government agencies, does not attract the brightest civilian engineering graduates, for it does not offer either the most lucrative or the most interesting engineering careers. The Corps work is largely what is known in the trade as "cookbook engineering." A ready-made formula is on hand for each problem. The Corps' bureaucracy draws heavily from the South, where the engineers who built the first dams and controlled the floods are still heroes.

The military patina gives the Corps its professional aura, its local popularity, its political success, and its independence. The military engineers are, as a group, polite, calm, and efficient, and their uniforms impress the politicians and the local citizens. The engineer who heads one of the Corps' forty district offices, usually a colonel, is a big man in his area; the newspapers herald his coming, and he is a star speaker at the Chamber of Commerce and Rotary lunches. But the military man gets transferred, so smart money also befriends the civilian officials in the district office. These men stay in the area, and want to see it progress. The Tulsa office of the Corps, for example, has about 1500 employees, of whom only three are military. The local offices are highly autonomous, for the Corps operates by the military principles that you never give a man an order he can't carry out, and that you trust your field commanders. If a district engineer believes strongly in a project, it is likely to get Corps endorsement. The Corps has mastered the art of convincing people that its projects are desirable, and so the projects are not examined very closely. Corps engineers are impressive in their command of details that non-engineers cannot understand, assiduous in publishing books that show what the Corps has done for each state, and punctilious about seeing that all the right politicians are invited to each dedication of a dam.

And so the Army Corps of Engineers has become one of the most independent bureaucracies in the federal government. The Corps' civil works section is neither of great interest to the Pentagon nor answerable to more relevant civilian bureaucracies. It makes its own living arrangements with the Congress, and deals not with the Armed Services Committees of the House and Senate, but with the Public Works Committees. Theoretically, the Corps reports to the appointed civilian chiefs of the Department of the Army, but these men are usually preoccupied with more urgent matters than Corps projects, and after a spell of trying to figure out what the Corps is doing, or even to control it, the civilians usually give up. "It was," said one man who tried not long ago, "like trying to round up the Viet Cong for an appearance on the *Lawrence Welk Show.*"

The power of the Corps stems from its relationships with Congress. It is the pet of the men from the areas it has helped the most, who also usually happen to be among the most senior and powerful members, and the ones on the committees which give the Corps its authority and its money. Thus, when the late Senator Robert Kerr of Oklahoma was a key member of the Senate Public Works Committee as well as the Senate Finance Committee, he devoted his considerable swashbuckling talents to winning final approval of a plan to build a navigation system stretching 450 miles from the Mississippi, up the Arkansas River, to Catoosa, Oklahoma, giving nearby Tulsa an outlet to the sea. The $1.2 billion project is said to be the largest since the Tennessee Valley Authority was built. The entire Oklahoma and Arkansas delegations, quarterbacked by a member of Kerr's staff, carried it through. The story goes that President Kennedy, having been advised to oppose the Arkansas River project, met with Kerr to seek his help on a tax bill. Kerr, not a very subtle man, told the President "I hope you understand how difficult I will find it to move the tax bill with the people of Oklahoma needing this river transportation." "You know, Bob," the President is said to have replied, "I think I understand the Arkansas River project for the first time." After Kerr's death, Senator John McClellan inherited the mantle of chief protector of the project, which reached the Arkansas-Oklahoma border last December, an event that was marked by a grand dedication.

The legislation that authorizes and appropriates the money for Corps projects encourages manipulation and swapping because of the unusual way in which it parcels out the money on a project-by-project basis. It is as if a housing bill had designated X dollars for a development here and Y dollars for a development there.

A very formal document—known around Capitol Hill as "eighteen steps to glory"—explains the procedures by which a project is initiated. In actuality, what happens is that local interests who stand to gain from a Corps project—barge companies, industrialists, contractors, real estate speculators—get together, often through the Chamber of Commerce, with the district engineer and ask for a project. The Corps literature is quite explicit about this: "When local interests feel that a need exists for any type of flood control, navigation or other improvement, it will be most profitable for them to consult at the outset with the District Engineer. He will provide full information as to what might be done to solve their particular problem, the authorities under which it might be accomplished, and the procedures necessary to initiate the action desired." Then the local groups ask their congressman, who is responsive to this particular segment of his constituency, to secure legislation authorizing the Corps to make a study of the project. Usually the Corps man is already aboard, but if not, he is not very far behind. "Sometimes," said a congressman who, like most of his colleagues, declined to be named when talking about the Corps, "the Chamber of Commerce will call me, and I'll say get in touch with Colonel So-and-so in the district office and he's over there like a shot; or the Corps will make an area survey and go to the community and drop hints that they might have a dam if they work on it." Frequently the project's promoters will form a group—the Mississippi Valley Association, the Tennessee-Tombigbee Association, the Arkansas Basin Development Association, and so on. The Florida Waterways Association, for example, boosters of the controversial Cross-Florida Barge Canal, has among its directors a realtor, representatives of a consulting engineering company, a dredging company, chambers of commerce, port authorities, newspapers, and a construction company. The associations meet and entertain and lobby. The Lower Mississippi Valley Association is noted for its days-long barge parties. Some twenty- to thirty-odd people from an association descend on Washington from time to time, to testify and to see the right people in Congress and the Executive Branch.

The power to authorize the study of a project, then to initiate it, and to appropriate the money for it is held by the Senate and House Public Works Committees, and by the Public Works Subcommittees of the Appropriations Committees of the two bodies. This is a total of seventy-one men; as is usual with congressional committees, a very few of the most senior men wield the key influence. It all comes down to a chess game played by the same players over the years—the committees, their staffs, and the Corps. There are always demands for more projects than can be studied, authorized, or financed, and so the Corps and the politicians are always in a position to do each other favors. One study can be moved ahead of another by the Corps if a man votes correctly. One project can get priority in the authorizing or appropriating stages. "Everyone is in everyone else's thrall," said a man who has been involved in the process, "unless he never wants a project."

The Corps has managed to arbitrate the demands for more projects than its budget can include through its highly developed sense of the relative political strengths within the Congress, and by making sure that each region of the country gets a little somehing each time. "We try to satisfy 10 per cent of the needs of each region," said a Corps official. From time to time, the Corps has been pressed by the Budget Bureau to recommend instead the most feasible projects in the nation as a whole, but the Corps has resisted this impolitic approach. The Secretary of the Army rarely changes the Corps' proposals. The Budget Bureau does examine the Corps' proposals on a project-by-project basis, but it runs a poor third to the Corps and Capitol Hill in deciding what the Corps program should be. The President, who is but a passerby, cannot establish control over the public works process unless he decides to make the kind of major political fight that Presidents usually do not think is worth it. On occasion, the White House will oppose a particularly outrageous project—or, out of political exigency, support one. Outsiders are unable to penetrate the continuing feedback between the Corps and the congressional committees, and are insufficiently informed to examine the rationale, the nature, and the alternatives of each project.

There may have been a Corps of Engineers project that was rejected on the floor of Congress, but no one can recall it. Every two years—in election years—a rivers and harbors and flood-control authorization bill is passed by Congress, and every year, money is appropriated. It has been calculated that, on the average, the authorization bills have provided something for 113 congressional districts (or more than one fourth of the House of Representatives) at a time, and the appropriations bills for 91 districts. "We used to say," said a man involved in the process, "that we could put our mortgage in that bill and no one would notice, and then the appropriations committees would cut it by 15 per cent." The most recent appropriation carried something for 48 states. On occasion, a senator, Paul Douglas of Illinois for one, or William Proxmire of Wisconsin for another, has spoken out against a particular Corps project, or the "pork-barrel" technique of legislating Corps projects, but they have not been taken seriously. "One hundred fifty-five million dollars has been spent as a starter," Proxmire once argued on the Senate floor in futile opposition to the Cross-Florida Barge Canal, "that is what it is, a starter—to make many more jobs, to make a great deal of money, and a great deal of profit. That is the essence of pork. That is why senators and congressmen fight for it and win re-election on it. Of course people who will benefit from these tens of millions of pork profit and jobs are in favor of it. That is perfectly natural and understandable. It will snow in Washington in July when a member of Congress arises and says spare my district the pork. What a day that will be."

Douglas fought rivers and harbors projects for years and then, in 1956, made a speech saying that he was giving up. "I think it is almost hopeless," he said, "for any senator to try to do what I tried to do when I first came to this body, namely, to consider these projects one by one. The bill is built up out of a whole system of mutual accommodations, in which the favors are widely distributed, with the implicit promise that no one will kick over the applecart; that if senators do not object to the bill as a whole, they will 'get theirs.' It is a process, if I may use an inelegant expression, of mutual back scratching and mutual logrolling. Any member who tries to buck the system is confronted with an impossible amount of work in trying to ascertain the relative merits of a given project."

The difficulty in understanding what a given Corps project will do, and what its merits are, comes not from a lack of material supplied by the Corps, but from an overabundance of it. A Corps report on a proposed project—the result of a survey that may take three to five years—is a shelf-long collection of volumes of technical material. Opponents of the project are on the defensive and unequipped to respond in kind.

Most of the projects that Congress asks the Corps to survey are, of course, turned down, because a congressman will pass along a request for a survey of almost anything. By the time a project moves through the Corps' bureaucracy to the Board of Engineers for Rivers and Harbors in Washington—what the Corps calls an "independent review group"—it has a promising future. The Board is made up of the Corps' various division engineers, who present their own projects and have learned to trust each other's judgment.

The supposedly objective standard for deciding whether a project is worthy of approval is the "benefit-to-cost" ratio. The potential benefits of a project are measured against the estimated costs, and the resulting ratio must be at least one-to-one—that is, one dollar of benefit for each dollar spent (the Corps prefers the term "invested")—to qualify. There is, however, considerable flexibility in the process, and at times the benefit-cost ratios of controversial projects are recomputed until they come out right. This was true of the Trinity River project to make Fort Worth a seaport, the Cross-Florida Barge Canal, and projects along the Potomac River. "There is enough room in the benefit-cost ratio," said a man who has worked with the Corps on Capitol Hill, "for the Corps to be responsive to strong members of Congress who really want a project." It has been remarked that the measurements are pliant enough to prove the feasibility of growing bananas on Pikes Peak.

There is much argument over the Corps' method of arriving at prospective benefits. For example, business that might be drawn by a project is considered among the benefits, even though there is no real way of knowing what business the project will attract and what the effects will be. The lower prices to a shipper of sending his goods by barge rather than by rail is also considered a national benefit; such a benefit may involve the fact that a wheat farmer is growing and shipping more wheat because of the lower prices, even though we do not need the wheat. The windfalls to real estate investors who have been lucky or clever enough to have bought inexpensive land—some of it underwater—in the path of a future project can turn up as a boon to us all in the form of "enhanced land values." The land, which can then be sold and developed for industrial, housing, or resort development, undergoes extraordinary value increases.

There are serious questions about how to estimate future benefits of flood control; the 1955 Hoover Commission report said that they are often "considerably overstated." In any event, in the three decades since the Flood Control Act was passed, annual losses due to floods have increased (in real prices). The apparent explanation is that the construction of flood-control dams, which cannot be built to guarantee protection against all manner of floods, do nevertheless encourage developers to build expensive properties on lands that will still be hit by floods. The protection of buildings which a flood-control dam attracts is counted as a national benefit, even though the buildings might have been built in a safer place, and there are less expensive ways to protect them. Antipollution treatment and hydroelectric power are counted as benefits even though there are cheaper ways of cleaning water and providing power. The benefits and costs are not compared with the benefits and costs of doing these things any other way. Promised benefits appear higher than they will turn out to be because of an unrealistic way of projecting the decline of the value of the dollar. Projected recreation benefits, which have accounted for an increasing proportion of the benefit to the nation from building these projects, are based on an assumption of how much people would be willing to pay for recreation privileges, even though they don't. The Corps lobbies to keep its parks free, in contrast to other national parks. The life of a project used to be estimated at 50 years in adding up the benefits; as fewer projects qualified, the Corps has simply shifted to a basis of 100 years. The cost of the loss of a wilderness, or a quiet river valley, is not deducted, there being no market value for that.

Since more projects are authorized than are given money to be begun, hundreds of them lie around for years, forgotten by all but the sponsors, or the sponsors' sons, and the Corps. If a project becomes too controversial, its backers can simply outwait the opponents. When old projects, sometimes thirty years old, are dusted off, they may be started without reconsideration of either the original purposes or the benefits and costs.

Once a project is begun, its costs almost invariably outrun the estimates (Table 1). Project proponents, on the other hand, argue that the benefits are consistently underestimated. The Corps is very sensitive about cost "overruns." They say that one must keep inflation in mind, and that such projects get changed and enlarged as they go along. Such changes, undermining the original benefit-cost rationale, do not seem to trouble the Congress. The Trinity River project, estimated at $790 million when it was authorized in 1962, is now expected to cost a little over $1 billion, and construction has not yet begun. The increases are not limited to the controversial projects. A look at project costs in a 1967 Corps report, the most recent one available, shows "overruns" of over 300 per cent.

Last year, despite a tight budget policy against "new starts," money to begin the Trinity River project was included in Lyndon Johnson's final budget, and was approved by the Congress. During most of his White House years, Mr. Johnson was sensitive about bestowing federal rewards upon Texas, which had benefited so handsomely from his congressional career. Nonetheless, in the end, he overcame his scruples. The fact that he did can be credited to the

Table 1   *Cost Increases on Corps Projects*

Name of Project	Cost Estimate at Time Project Was Authorized	Amount Spent Through Fiscal Year 1966	Percentage Overrun
Whitney (Tex.)	$ 8,350,000	$ 41,000,000	391%
John H. Kerr (N.C. & Va.)	30,900,000	87,733,000	185
Blakely Mountain (Ark.)	11,080,000	31,500,000	184
Oahe Reservoir (N. & S. Dak.)	72,800,000	334,000,000	359
Jim Woodruff (Fla.)	24,139,000	46,400,000	92
Chief Joseph (Wash.)	104,050,000	144,734,000	39
Fort Peck (Mont.)	86,000,000	156,859,000	82
Clark Hill (Ga. & S.C.)	28,000,000	79,695,000	185
Bull Shoals (Ark.)	40,000,000	88,824,000	122

persistence, and the excellent connections, of the Texas lobbyists for the project.

The major purpose of the Trinity project is to build a navigable channel from the Fort Worth-Dallas area 370 miles to the Gulf of Mexico. Like many other projects, this one has been boosted for a long, long time. It is said that Will Rogers was brought down to Texas once to make a speech in behalf of the Trinity, which is barely wet during some of the year. "I think you're right," Rogers told the Trinity Improvement Association, "I think you ought to go ahead and pave it." There have been a number of restudies of the feasibility of the Trinity project. At first it was justified on the basis of the shipping of wheat. The current justification assures a great deal of shipping of gravel, although there is some question as to the need to ship gravel from one end of Texas to the other. "It's the wildest scheme I ever saw," said a Texas politician who dared not be quoted. "They have to dig every foot of it. Then they have to put expensive locks in. You could put five railroads in for that price. I'm not carrying any brief for the railroads. You could put in a railroad and make the government pay for every inch of it and call it the United States Short Line and save a hell of a lot of money."

The Trinity River will feed barge traffic into another Texas-based waterways scheme, the Gulf Intracoastal Canal, which, when completed, will run from Brownsville, Texas, on the Mexican border, to the west coast of Florida. From there it will link up with the Cross-Florida Barge Canal, and then another channel all the way to Trenton, New Jersey. This has given the whole network a great deal of backing, which comes together in Washington through the efforts of Dale Miller, a long-time representative of a number of Texas interests. Miller, a white-haired, soft-spoken Texan came to town in 1941 with his ambitious, ebullient wife, Scooter, and took up his father's work in promoting projects for Texas. Miller represents the Gulf Intracoastal Canal Association, the Port of Corpus Christi, the Texas Gulf Sulphur Company, and the Chamber of Commerce of Dallas, for which the Trinity project is "the number-one program." He is also the vice president of the Trinity Improvement Association. ("So I have a direct interest in the Trinity at both ends.")

From the time they arrived in Washington, Dale and Scooter Miller played bridge almost every weekend with the young Corps lieutenants who lived at Fort Belvoir, just outside Washington, and now they are "good friends" with the important members of the Corps. "We move in military social circles," says Miller. "We have them to our parties, and they have us to theirs." The Millers also moved in Washington's political circles, and were close friends of Lyndon and Lady Bird Johnson's, and other powerful Washingtonians. Miller was the chairman of Johnson's inauguration in 1965. But he and his wife had the good sense to maintain bipartisan contacts. Last year they gave a large party that was described in the social pages as "50-50 Democrats and Republicans." Miller says that the coming of a Republican Administration has not hindered his work: "I just put on a more conservative tie, and I'm still in business." He works out of a suite in the Mayflower Hotel, its rooms filled with photographs of Johnson and Sam Rayburn, a harp, and a painting of the Dale Miller Bridge over the Intracoastal Canal in Corpus Christi. "It gives me an opportunity for that wonderful line," says Miller, " 'I'm not too big for my bridges.' "

Miller is also president and chairman of the board of the National Rivers and Harbors Congress, an unusual lobbying organization made up of politicians and private interests who support federal water projects. The chairman emeritus of the Rivers and Harbors Congress is Senator John McClellan. Among its directors are Senators Allen Ellender of Louisiana (chairman of the Public Works Appropriations Subcommittee) and Ralph Yarborough of Texas, and Congressmen Hale Boggs of Louisiana and Robert Sikes of Florida. Other officers of the group represent industries which use water transportation for their bulk cargo—such as Ashland Oil, farmers, and the coal business—and the Detroit Harbor and dredging companies. The resident executive director in Washington is George Gettinger, an elderly Indianan who has been in and out of a number of businesses and was a founder of the Wabash Valley Association, and "learned from my cash register" the value of federal water projects. "Your directors of your churches have businesses," says Gettinger, "your trustees of your universities have businesses. Sure our people make a living in water resources, just like other people. So help me, it's time we sat down and started looking at the benefits that have derived from this program. It's one of the bright spots in solving the population problem. It has settled people along rivers so they don't have to live in the inner city. The ghettos in this country are something it's not good to live with."

In its pursuit of a solution to the urban crisis, the Rivers and Harbors Congress meets every year in Washington, at the Mayflower Hotel. Its members discuss their mutual interests and then fan out about town to talk to politicians and government officials. There is a projects committee which chooses priorities among the various proposed projects. "It asks the federal agencies about the projects," explains Gettinger. "Until the Rivers and Harbors Congress there was no kind of national clearance. Their endorsement has meant so much because it comes from a group that serves without pay." The project committee holds hearings at each convention, and then it adjourns to Dale Miller's suite to decide the public works priorities. As it turns out, the projects that are mainly for navigation receive the most support. "We have no axes to grind," says Miller. "We're just in favor of development of water resources."

The nationwide coalition of interested groups keeps the momentum behind the public works program, and gives the barge industry, probably the program's largest single beneficiary, and an important national industry some seventy-five years ago, the strength to continue to win its federal largesse. Besides working with the Rivers and Harbors Congress, the barge companies have their own trade associations, which have warded off tolls for the use of the federally constructed waterways.

The only major group that opposes most Corps projects is the railroad industry, which inevitably resists federally subsidized competition. On occasion, it succeeds. It is generally believed, for example, that the railroads, working through the Pennsylvania state government, blocked "Kirwan's ditch," a controversial project named after Mike Kirwan of Ohio, the chairman of the House Public Works Appropriations Subcommittee. At a cost of almost $1 billion, "Kirwan's ditch" was to link Lake Erie and the Ohio River.

The railroads also opposed the Trinity River project, but they did not succeed. Trinity had too much going for it: Jim Wright, a congressman from Fort Worth and a friend of President Johnson's, is a senior member of the House Public Works Committee. Dale Miller, with valuable assistance from Marvin Watson when Watson was the President's appointments secretary and later when he was the Postmaster General, was able to help the representatives of the Trinity Improvement Association get a sympathetic hearing from all the important people, including the President. Balky officials were called into Postmaster General Watson's office to be persuaded of the value of the Trinity project.

Watson, as Miller put it, had "great familiarity with water projects in the Southwest." He had worked for the Red River Valley Association, and the Chamber of Commerce of Daingerfield, Texas, and then Lone Star Steel, which is located just outside Daingerfield. Watson had been a major force in securing, with the help of then Senator Johnson, a Corps water project which left Lone Star Steel with water and several of the surrounding little towns with higher taxes to pay off bonds which they had approved, in the mistaken impression that they too could draw water from the project. (It was later determined that they were too far away, and Watson became a very controversial figure in East Texas.) Watson maintained his efforts on behalf of the Red River Valley projects after he took up official positions in Washington. The Red River navigation project, to build a waterway from Daingerfield, Texas, to the Mississippi River, was authorized in 1968 to go as far as Shreveport.

After many years of success, Dale Miller's projects, like so many others, are now coming under fire because of what they will do to the environment. There is a "missing link" between the Gulf Intracoastal Canal and the Cross-Florida Barge Canal on the long way from Brownsville, Texas, to Trenton, New Jersey. The link has been authorized, but construction is being opposed. A navigation channel from Miami to Trenton already exists. "That doesn't carry a tremendous amount of tonnage," Miller says, "but it carries a tremendous amount of recreational traffic, people in their yachts and everything.

"The problem which all developers—which we are—now face is the growing awareness of environmental problems. I mean ecological change. It's a very difficult area because we don't know too much about it—what effects dredging will have on baby shrimp, or marine life. It cuts both ways. We had developed that whole Gulf part of it before anyone raised the question of the effects. Nature is much more resilient than people think it is. In dredging, you may disturb an estuary where baby shrimp and marine life were, but it didn't mean permanent destruction, just change. They were breeding somewhere else in a year. In this missing link we're going to have to satisfy the ecologists in advance, and it's going to be very difficult. I'm convinced that the developers and the preservationists are not as far apart as people think. I think the difference can be reconciled and then we can move even faster. The problem a lot of us have, paraphrasing the little-old-ladies-in-tennis-shoes approach, is that we're not dealing with the knowledgeable and experienced people in ecology, but the bird watchers and butterfly-net people who don't want anything changed anywhere, and you can't deal with them."

As the country runs out of choice land near the cities, the solution has been to fill in the adjacent waterways. Besides what such schemes do to the scenery, it is now beginning to be understood what they do to natural life. Estuaries, or those places where rivers meet the sea, provide a special balance of salt and fresh water that is essential to certain fish, such as oysters and shrimp. They also provide food and habitats for waterfowl. The damming of rivers has also damaged estuarine life. Local governments are often willing to have the estuaries dredged and filled, for this raises the real estate values, and hence the local tax base. One third of San Francisco Bay, for example, has already been filled in, most of it for airport runways, industrial parks, and areas proposed for residential subdivisions. "It is conceivable," said Congressman Paul McCloskey, who had fought for conservation as a lawyer before coming to Congress in 1967, "that by 1990 the filling of shallow waters of the Bay could reduce it to the status of a river across which our grandchildren will be skipping rocks."

In response to criticism of its easiness with granting land-fill permits, and to a recent federal requirement that the Corps consider the effects on fish and wildlife, the Corps has begun to deny some permits. One such denial, however, was challenged in court, and a district judge in Florida ruled that the Corps did not have discretion to deny a permit on any grounds other than that it would impede navigation. The case is still in the courts. The Corps argues, with some validity, that it should not be making zoning decisions for local governments. "This points up the fact," said McCloskey, "that some new national land-use authority must be created which will have the power to put federal zoning on waterways, historic sites, and land areas of particular national significance." Such a policy would protect such areas as the Everglades. Congressman Richard Ottinger of New York, also a man interested in conservation before it became fashionable, has been pushing legislation to require that the effects on the environment must be taken into account in any federal program which contributes to construction or issues licenses—the Corps, airport and highway programs, and so on.

The Corps of Engineers public works program has been, among other things, an income-transfer program, and this is a good time to look more closely at who has been transferring what to whom. The federal government has been paying for the Corps program—or rather, all of the taxpayers have. And the Corps program consists in the main of subsidies for irrigation, navigation, and flood control. Some projects have been for the benefit of only one particular industry. Former Senator Douglas has charged, for example, that a project to deepen the Detroit River was for the benefit of the Detroit Edison Company alone, and that a project to deepen the Delaware River from Philadelphia to Trenton was to serve one mill of the United States Steel Corporation, which was quite able to pay for the project itself. An industry or developer builds on a flood plain and then asks the federal government to save it from floods. A wild river is converted for use by an industry; subsequently a federal subsidy is given to clean up the industry's pollution of the river. The barge industry is kept afloat because it is there.

Robert Haveman, an economist and author of *Water Resource Investment and the Public Interest,* has shown that the preponderance of Corps projects has gone to three regions: the South and Southwest, the Far West, and North and South Dakota, but mainly to the South, in particular the lower Mississippi River area. Within an area, the rewards are not evenly spread. The major beneficiaries of the flood-control projects which also provide water for irrigation have been the large landholders—in particular, in the Mississippi Delta and San Joaquin Valley. These are the same landowners who are paid the largest federal farm subsidies for not growing the crops which the federal water projects make it possible for them to grow. The Corps is still preparing to produce more farmland, in the name of flood control, in the Mississippi Delta region.

The Corps, in a publication called "The Army Engineers' Contributions to American Beauty," notes: "In Dallas, the flood-control project for channeling the flood waters of the Trinity River through the center of town (once some of the least desirable real estate in the city) is being made into a long, winding stretch of parkway. In Los Angeles and other Pacific Coast cities built below mountain slopes, the development of attractive and sometimes luxurious residential areas has been made possible by Army Engineer projects which curb flash floods."

The Corps established an environmental division a few years ago, to advise on the environmental effects of its projects. This summer it is sponsoring a seminar on how it can better "communicate" with the public. Corps officials have been urging greater environmental concerns on the Corps members, and on their clientele, appealing, among other things, to their self-interest. In a recent speech, Major General F. P. Koisch, director of the Corps' Civil Works Division, told the Gulf Intracoastal Canal Association to listen to "the voice of the so-called 'New Conservation.'

"By and large," he said, "its advocates oppose the old concepts of expansion and development. Yet they are not merely negative, for they are willing to lavish huge sums on programs which embody their own conceptions of natural resource management. Their theories and concepts are not always consistent nor fully worked out. They are less concerned with means than with ends and goals—their vision of a better America. But they do seem to represent an idea whose time has come. So it grows clearer every day that it is up to us, who like to think of ourselves as scientific, practical men who know how to get things done, to make this new idea our own and make it work. . . . This can open a whole new career for the Gulf Intracoastal Canal Association. . . . This business of ecology," says General

Koisch, "we're concerned, but people don't know enough about it to give good advice. You have to stand still and study life cycles, and we don't have time. We have to develop before 1980 as much water resource development as has taken place in the whole history of the nation."

"It is a fact," said General Richard H. Groves, his deputy, in a speech, "that our nation is engaged in a struggle to survive its technology and its habits. It is a fact, too, that we are defiling our waters, polluting our air, littering our land, and infecting our soil and ourselves with the wastes which our civilization produces. These are serious problems, but we cannot permit ourselves to yield to an emotional impulse that would make their cure the central purpose of our society. Nor is there any reason why we should feel guilty about the alterations which we have to make in the natural environment as we meet our water-related needs."

In an interview, General Groves said he did not believe that the basic role of the Corps would change. "Certainly, parts of it will. One part that is obvious is control of pollution, control of the ecology, which is more or less the same. There are very heavy pressures that have developed, and nobody in this business can ignore them. We would hope that in responding to these pressures we don't lose sight of the need to keep everything in perspective. The program keeps growing. The program as you know is tied to people, and the people double every forty years. . . . We build the program," he said —and here is the heart of it all—"on the notion that people want an ever-increasing standard of living, and the standard of living is tied to water programs. If you conserve underdeveloped areas, you're not going to be able to do it. If you double the population and they double their standard of living, you have to keep going. It's not as simple as the people who take an extreme view say."

Clearly, no rational settlement of the conflict between "progress" and the environment is going to come from dam-by-dam fights between the Corps and the conservationists. The conservationists have been out there all alone all these years, and they have worked hard, but they have lacked a national strategy. In some instances, they have tried to have it all ways: opposing not only hydroelectric projects but also alternatives such as generating power through burning fuels (air pollution) or building a nuclear plant (thermal pollution and radiation hazards). Some conservationists have been interested in "preserving" the wildlife so that they could shoot it.

Where engineers have been pitted against engineers, as in the case of the Oakley and Potomac dams, the opponents have been more successful. "The only way to resist," says Representative John Saylor of Pennsylvania, a critic of the Corps for years, "is to know a little more about the Corps than the Chambers of Commerce do." The new approach of trying to build a body of law on the basis of the "rights of the people" against a public works project could be of profound importance.

Some water economists have suggested quite seriously a ten-year moratorium on water projects. There is an ample supply of water, they say. Problems arise where industries use it inefficiently because it is provided so cheaply, and pollute much of it. The answer for the pollution, the experts say, is sewage treatment at the point where the pollution originates.

So one solution to the problems the Corps program creates would be simply to stop it. The Corps and the Public Works Committees and the river associations could give themselves a grand testimonial dinner, congratulate themselves on their good works, and go out of business. There are more effective ways of transferring money—for instance, directly—if that is what we want to do; there are others who need the money more. But such suggestions are not, of course, "practical."

For as long as anyone can remember, there have been proposals for removing the public works program from the military, and transferring the Corps' civil functions, or at least the planning functions, to the Interior Department or a new department dealing with natural resources. President Nixon considered similar ideas, but rejected them in preparing his message on the environment. The Corps likes being where it is, and the powerful Forest Service and Soil Conservation Service, which are secure in the Agriculture Department, and the congressional committees whose power derives from the present arrangements, have habitually and successfully resisted up to now. "The two most powerful intragovernmental lobbies in Washington are the Forest Service and the Army Engineers," wrote FDR's Interior Secretary Harold Ickes in his diary in 1937, in the midst of a vain effort to reorganize them and Interior into a new Department of Conservation. Whatever the chances for reform, it has never been clear who would be swallowing whom as a result of such a change. The closed-circuit system by which public works decisions are made should be opened to other interested parties. Certainly a federal program that is more than a century old should be overhauled. The Corps is now at work on some internal improvements, but bureaucracies are not notably rigorous about self-change, and the water interests do not want change.

If there are to be a Corps and a Corps public works program, then proposals to expand the Corps' functions make sense. Making the Corps responsible for sewage treatment, for example, would give it a task that needs to be done, local governments a benefit which they really need and which would be widely shared, and politicians a new form of largesse to hand around. Antipollution could be spared the pork barrel through a combination of requirements for local action and federal incentives, and through adequate financing. Yet making antipollution part of the pork barrel may be just what it needs. Programs which appeal to greed are notably more politically successful than those that do not. The Corps' engineering expertise, in any event, could be put to use for something other than building dams and straightening rivers. It is the judgment of just about every economist who has studied the public works program that there should be cost-sharing and user charges. There have been proposals for making the beneficiaries of flood-control and navigation projects and harbors pay for them, or at least part of them.

In a period of great needs and limited resources, a high proportion of the public works program amounts to inefficient expenditures and long-range commitments of money on behalf of those who make the most noise and pull the most strings. Despite all the talk about "reordering priorities," the Nixon Administration's budget for the next year increases the money for the Corps. Even if the nation should want to double its standard of living (leaving aside for the moment the question of whose standard of living) and even if the public works programs really could help bring that about, it would be good to know more about the nature and price of such a commitment. At a time when a number of our domestic arrangements are coming under re-examination, this one is a prime candidate for reform. Meanwhile, the changes it is making in the nation are irreversible.

Projects

1.   Research the origin of the phrase "pork-barrel project." Report your findings to the class.

2.   Read Joseph Wood Krutch's book, *The Voice of the Desert* (Apollo Editions, 1966) or John Storer's *The Web of Life* (Signet Science Library Books, 1956). Report to your class some of the complex interrelationships between animal and plant life and the environment. Consider the destruction that a large-scale project, such as a Corps dam, would have on these ancient relationships.

3.   Investigate the proposed North American Water and Power Alliance, the Corps' most grandiose plan. Report it to your class.

4.   Mrs. Drew points out the difficulties of defeating plans by federal bureaucracies such as the Corps. However, in the late 1960s, national conservation groups prevented construction of two new dams on the Colorado River (H.R. 4671). One of the dams planned by the U. S. Bureau of Reclamation, Bridge Canyon Dam, would have been in the lower Grand Canyon between Lake Mead and Grand Canyon National Monument. The other dam would have been in Marble Canyon, twelve miles upstream from Grand Canyon National Park. Study this conservation battle, noting the strategies used. Compare them to the methods Leopold discusses in "The Land Ethic." Write a paper reviewing the lessons conservationists might learn from this success.

Suggested Topics for Writing

1.   The official history of the Corps of Engineers asserts that "the power of Engineering Character, Engineering Leadership, and Engineering Knowledge" is "America's greatest power." Explore the degree to which this "power" is responsible for our present environmental crisis.

2.   General Koisch of the Corps is quoted as saying, "You have to stand still and study life cycles, and we don't have time." Write a letter of rebuttal to General Koisch. Point out the dangers of this attitude. Support your generalizations by reference to problems that have resulted from projects designed without sufficient ecological information.

3.   Discuss an example of mismanagement of your community environment because of dependence on an outmoded bureaucracy.

Exercises

1. Comment on the appropriateness of the title, "Dam Outrage: the Story of the Army Engineers."

2. As Mrs. Drew reports the story of the Army engineers, she frequently uses quotations. Who are the speakers? How does use of quotations affect the objectivity of the report? What impressions do you form of the various speakers?

3. Consider generalizations made by speakers quoted in the report. Who are the "bird watchers and butterfly-net people"? Do they, in truth, not want anything changed anywhere? Is nature "much more resilient than people think it is"? Is control of pollution "more or less the same thing" as control of ecology? Can ecology be controlled? Is conservation merely "an idea whose time has come"? Is "the power of Engineering Character, Engineering Leadership, and Engineering Knowledge" "America's greatest power"?

4. The quotation from Senator Douglas' congressional speech contains several metaphors. Are they effective? Why or why not?

5. "Low-flow augmentation" is a euphemism the Corps uses when referring to the practice of diluting sewage poured into public waterways. What function does the euphemism serve?

6. What are the duties of the Corps of Engineers? List the ways in which the Corps has benefited our nation.

7. Explain the "cost-benefit-ratio." What weaknesses are inherent in this method of computing the value of a project?

8. Why is the Corps now such an independent organization?

9. What steps might be taken to resolve the conflicts existing between various federal bureaucracies charged with managing our national environment?

26. Sopris, Colorado: Requiem for a Small Town

NANCY WOOD

The death of a small town in America does not count for much. Small towns succumb to dams, farms to factories, forests to subdivisions; wilderness depreciates into real estate, mountains are divided by interstate highways, and wild rivers learn to mind their manners.

On the bank of the Purgatoire River in southeastern Colorado there is a town called Sopris that will die this New Year's Eve, when Catherine Maccagnan will serve the last drink over her orange, black, and green bar; when the power will be shut off, the last good-bys said, and Sopris will surrender to the U.S. Army Corps of Engineers. The bulldozers will come to knock down what is left of the town, and by and by a giant earth-filled dam made from the streets and fields and back yards of Sopris will restrain the temperamental Purgatoire, once known as *El Río de Las Animas Perdidas en Purgatorio*—The River of Souls Lost in Purgatory. By 1975 one hundred feet of water will cover the place where four generations of Italian-American coal miners have lived and labored and loved.

Sopris has had no important history, no significant architecture. It produced no famous men, no great thinkers, no millionaires. The Indians never bothered it, the gold prospectors passed it by, the homesteaders refused it. But the water politicians coveted it, and the only people who cared about Sopris were the people who lived there.

In 1885, when the steam engines were pulling long freight loads over Raton Pass toward Trinidad five miles east of Sopris and the wagons were still rolling nearby along the Santa Fe Trail, the new Sopris mine produced more coal than any other camp in Las Animas County. By World War I, nearly two thousand people, mostly immigrant Italians, lived in Sopris and the three adjoining communities. They came from the old country to join their friends and relatives in this isolated coal camp that became as Italian as the towns they had left.

They married among themselves generation after generation, until so many of them shared the same family names that the church records read like a litany. A Maccagnan married a Cunico, another Cunico married an Incitti, the Regusas became related to the Terrys, two Sebben brothers married two Terry sisters, a De Angelis married a nonrelated De Angelis, two Liras married yet two more Cunicos, and on and on in a multiplication of relationships unfactorable by any outsider.

When the last Sopris mine shut down in 1940, the population dwindled rapidly. By the time the Army Corps of Engineers arrived in 1967 to begin the two-hundred-foot-high dam tower that already looms above the town, Sopris had about three hundred people, most of them pensioners.

Fifty years ago there was talk of a dam, because the Purgatoire goes on a rampage once every five years or so and floods nearby Trinidad, population ten thousand. The river drops eight thousand feet in seventy-five miles, and dozens of small streams swell and feed into it when it rains, so the Purgatoire sometimes descends with a wall of water and no warning. The river also floods because the giant Colorado Fuel and Iron Corporation, which owns all of the coal mines and much of the landscape around Sopris, has been careless with the watershed. "They cut trees up there till hell wouldn't have it," remembers Paul Butero, who retired with black lung disease after forty years in the mines.

For years the government men came and went, survey after survey was taken, and Congress finally voted the dam, convinced that the benefits outweighed the $55,000,000 cost. The only casualty was the little town of Sopris.

Because Sopris never bothered to incorporate, the government did not have to build new houses for the people or move them to a new location. They were simply paid a sum of money for their places and told to move, and their homes were bulldozed into piles of rubble, which still remain. If the people didn't want to leave they could lease back the homes they had built with their own hands and stay a little while longer.

A few refused to accept the government's price and saw their property condemned. A few wrote to Washington and received courteous, intractable answers. A few fought with the government appraiser and claim they got less for their houses because they did. And a few, it is said, died on purpose rather than pack up and leave.

One peppery resident of Sopris, eighty-two-year-old Frances Furia, sat in her living room one afternoon near the end, surrounded by framed photographs of her huge family. She had lived in that house for fifty-five years, the wife of a miner-shoemaker-barber now dead and the mother of twelve children. Shaking her head, she snapped, "They spend millions on that dam. What advantage is it? Flood control they say. Well there is a house down there on the river bottom where they raised fifteen kids and I said to the engineer how come it didn't float away? But what you going to do? Fight? Kill 'em? Then you go to jail. You argue with them they give you less money for the house.

"This was a pretty camp. A band every Saturday night. I'd go outside and listen. It was like a city—two coal mines, a coke oven, and a streetcar until they took it out and we had to walk to town like nanny goats.

"Oh, maybe no dam will ever come. I think they are all *pazzo*," which means "crazy" and is accompanied by an appropriate gesture.

Crazy or not, the people who like the dam say that it will save the town of Trinidad from floods and enhance the area with a twenty-five-mile-long lake for recreation. But others say that the last two times Trinidad was flooded the water came from a tributary downriver from the dam; that the mountainous slag heaps left over from the mines will dissolve fish-killing acid into the lake; that the Purgatoire's water is muddy and fit only for junk fish; and that an eighty-six-foot seasonal drawdown will expose an ugly bathtub ring of mud flats to further discourage recreation.

Now that the decision is final and the dam is imminent, the last wish of the Sopris people is that the dam and reservoir be named after their town instead of Trinidad. "After all," said Joe Terry, sitting in the house his wife's grandfather built and drinking some twelve-year-old muscatel his wife's grandfather made, "Sopris has lost its life, and there is Trinidad with its name on the tombstone."

But in the end Sopris will surrender to progress with dignity and without self-pity, perhaps because for eighty-five years Sopris, lacking progress, has survived on laughter and love and close ties with large and extended families and *compari,* those for whom one feels fraternal responsibility.

When a Sopris tavern burned down one Thanksgiving Day, the owner's *compari* had him back in business by New Year's Eve. When a man was out of work for six months, loaves of bread appeared on his table. The Sopris grocery stores stayed almost broke feeding their own.

The modest houses were built mostly of adobe or wood and stucco, and they grew as the families grew, with a plot reserved for vegetables and flowers and another for the brick ovens where the women baked the *pane.*

Some men died in the mines or were crippled, and many got black lung from breathing the coal dust, so they coughed and spit and were forever out of breath. In the old days a man got three dollars a day for digging sixteen tons of coal with a pick and a shovel, and he did not see the light of day except on Sundays. The men worked in the mine alongside their mules, and if his mule died in the mine, a man was fired on the spot; but when a man got killed he was left on the crosscut until the shift ended.

The poverty was endless, but they did not know until they grew up how poor they were, because they had the hills to climb for piñon nuts, the streams to fish for trout, the slag heap to ride a shovel down in winter, and the Sangre de Cristo Mountains thirty miles west to hunt for deer. And they had each other in an unself-conscious sort of way.

Beneath the houses the men established their wine cellars, and every fall when the grapes came from California each man made the wine in his own way, some with sugar, some without, some adding heat and others letting the mash ferment in its own good time, some crushing the grapes with their feet as their fathers had done in the old country.

The wine was important to them. Even when the men cut up tires and fastened pieces to their children's shoes to replace the worn-out soles, there was somehow always money for grapes. They say in

Sopris that as long as they had the wine they felt lucky, and they drink a toast that goes, "A hundred years and then you die," and they insist that three glasses are a minimum and that a drop spilled is a drop you do not get to drink.

Because making the wine and drinking it together are secular sacraments to them, they are very careful with it. Joe Terry, at twenty-nine, is the only one of his generation making wine. In the cellar of his Sopris house are about one hundred gallons of muscatel and zinfandel quietly aging in the oaken barrels used by his grandfather. "The one thing I hate about leaving," he said, "is that my wine barrels have to get stood up."

The people who still live in Sopris or nearby sit around kitchen tables and drink the wine, remembering when the place was good and the people were a part of one another and the spirit that united them ran as strong as the wine.

A celebration was held prematurely on the Fourth of July so six hundred Sopris people who had moved away could come back for a final farewell.

The day before the event the cars streamed up from Trinidad, crossed the rusting iron truss bridge, dodged the potholes in the neglected road, and headed single file for Catherine Maccagnan's tavern in the shadow of the reinforced-concrete tower that prefigures the dam. The tavern is worn and plain, without a sign to announce it, but it is known for miles around as "Catherine's place" or "Katie's." Inside, there isn't much besides the long mirrored bar, "the only black, green, and orange bar in the world"; a few booths along the opposite wall, with local scenes by an itinerant artist painted on triangular panels above; a high embossed-tin ceiling from which descends a single electric fan; family pictures stuck up above the ancient cash register; a juke box, a pool table, and a few pinball machines. Everyone drinks at the bar, presided over by Catherine for thirty-five of her sixty-five years. She doesn't look her age, but that night she proudly claimed, "It took two thousand years to produce this face," as the beer ran like water, the hail beat down on the roof, and the crowd sang loud and off key the same as always.

The next day dawned bright and clear with a freshness in the air following the night's rain. All along the road to Sopris hand-lettered signs were nailed to trees and posts: GOD IS ALIVE AND WELL IN SOPRIS; DAMN THE DAM; SMILE, YOU ARE IN SOPRIS; YOU CAN TAKE THE PEOPLE OUT OF SOPRIS BUT YOU CAN'T TAKE SOPRIS OUT

OF THE PEOPLE; and at the church, THIS CHURCH IS STILL USED—DO NOT DAMAGE—THANK YOU. Inside was a banner draped from the choir loft that said: FATHER JIM MADE TODAY—THANK YOU FATHER, because the person most responsible for the idea and for making it work was Father Jim Koenigsfeld, a twenty-seven-year-old from Iowa who came to the adobe church only two years ago fresh from his ordination.

The families came with lunch baskets and coolers and picnicked in front of their old homes. Salvage men who had bought up some of the old houses for scrap arrived during lunch, and the sounds of demolition punctuated the laughter. One old miner said in mid-afternoon, "They just took away the porch I was eating on."

The old men stood arm in arm under the cottonwoods and the elms, glancing up at a jet streaking across a brittle blue sky and the sun gleaming on Fisher's Peak away to the east, drinking beer and speaking their mother tongue. Shorty D'Ercole, eighty years old, stood with Pop Incitti, who is seventy-six. Both are under five feet tall, both worked all their lives in the mines, and both have faces that have come from the earth. The two old men danced together in the gym, played *boccie,* and talked of old times. Shorty said to Pop, waving his hands excitedly as though it were happening then, "The mules, remember the mules in the mine that was caving in? There was the lead mule, that red one with a face like a horse, in there tangled up in the chains. And I said please somebody get out the mules, and they were making the noise and scraping the feet and I couldn't stand it and I went in and brought them out. Then the whole thing collapsed." The two old men laughed and went down the street together.

Crist Cunico went into the mines at fourteen and came out fifty years later, though his face is unlined and young and he appears to have spent all his life outdoors. His son, like most Sopris children, was sent to school instead of into the mines. Crist, Jr., is thirty-eight and has a degree in electrical engineering. He stood with his arm around his own small son and suddenly bent down and kissed him. "There's something here that can't be replaced," he said. "We climbed those hills as kids. We had our first loves here . . . I've been in sixteen foreign countries and forty states and I make a good living in Tulsa, but I'd give it all up to come back here to live and die and be buried."

When all the beer was gone, when the band stopped playing

and the people began to leave, Pop Incitti went to his new home in Trinidad carrying a lump of coal awarded to him for being the oldest miner at the celebration, because Shorty D'Ercole went home early. He went to his cellar, drew a bottle of wine from the cool sand, and his dark eyes danced and a grin spread across his weathered face. "The wine is still good," he said. "The wine you can still make. The wine you can take with you." And by and by he got out his old accordion and began to play the old songs, and his family sang with him and drank his wine. After a while the old man stopped playing and took a pencil and wrote a poem in Italian about the end of Sopris. One line went: "We will leave all the roses to rest beneath the water."

Before the celebration there was a Mass. From the back of the church a procession of Sopris people came to the altar bearing the things for the Offertory: a loaf of freshly baked bread in a basket woven by Pop Incitti, a bottle of wine, a columbine, a miner's helmet, a lump of coal on a silver tray.

A priest read from Ecclesiastes:

To every thing there is a season, and
    a time to every purpose under the
    heaven:
A time to be born, and a time to die . . .
    . . . a time to break down, and a time to
    build up;
A time to weep, and a time to laugh;
A time to mourn, and a time to dance. . . .

After the Mass an old woman came out of a house nearby, shooing the chickens, and said, "Be sure and have a dance so when you're old like me you can come back with a fishing pole and say, down there is where I had a dance."

Projects

1.   Read *The Place No One Knew: Glen Canyon* by Eliot Porter. The book, which contains eighty color photographs, is a requiem for a single canyon on the Colorado. The canyon was flooded when the Colorado River was dammed. Or read *Goodbye to a River* by John Graves, a moving account of one man's last canoe trip down the

Brazos River in West Central Texas, before engineers killed it with dams. Report on the experience of reading the book.

2. Engineers claim that the dam at Sopris will provide recreation as well as flood control. Other dams are said to provide hydroelectric power, irrigation water, and low-flow augmentation in addition to flood control and recreation. Critics of these "multipurpose" projects claim that dams cannot adequately serve such diverse purposes. Investigate the arguments for and against multipurpose dams. Discuss your findings with your class.

Exercises

1. Examine the purpose and tone of the essay. Has the author glamorized Sopris, its people, their way of life?

2. Particularly consider use of detail. The author has not related all the events that occurred during the Fourth of July celebration. What criteria seem to have governed the selection of detail?

3. Relying on background from the essay, "Dam Outrage," explain the phrase, "water politicians."

4. What is a "watershed"? What kinds of mismanagement impair a watershed?

5. A former resident of Sopris reports that as a child he did not know he was poor. Consider the life of the rural poor and that of the urban poor. Are they significantly different? What aspects of his life probably enabled the Sopris youth to disregard his poverty?

6. The author comments that "the only casualty of the dam was the little town of Sopris." Consider the Trinidad dam project from an ecological point of view. Will Sopris be the "only casualty"? Using maps and geographic accounts, study the southern Colorado terrain through which the Purgatoire River runs. What kinds of changes will a dam and reservoir introduce into this area?

27. *Weeds, Bugs, Americans*

JOHN FOWLES

One thing I like about Zen philosophy is its mean attitude to words. It doesn't trust them. As soon as we have a thing named, says Zen, we start forgetting about its real nature. So labels, especially labels for very common human problems, tend to become convenient excuses for letting the problems take care of themselves. The particular stinking corpse buried beneath a word that I have in mind here is conservation.

No public figure today would dare state that he thinks humanity *can* support the continued cost of pollution and dying nature. Never mind what the public figure may do in private practice, he won't deny the most fashionable solicitude of our time. We all agree we need conservation. It is national policy, state policy, local policy, everybody's policy. And with all that interest and public concern it's very clear that you and I don't have to do a thing about it—except pay lip service to the general principle. Very much the same self-excusing process has overtaken charity. A hundred years ago charity was still mainly a private matter. Now it has become a function—and very often a cautious diplomatic calculation—of elected government.

Reprinted by permission of Julian Bach Literary Agency, Inc. Copyright © 1970 Time Inc.

The actual experience of direct charity, the reality of giving to a stranger in need, has been lost. The charitably inclined private citizen finds himself faced with just one more of those countless pressing invitations to do nothing that our century has been so fertile in devising.

There is a story about Samuel Rogers, the British poet who was a contemporary of Byron and Shelley. At one of his literary dinners a group of friends were holding forth on the iniquities of slavery. For hours they poured out their fine liberal sentiments. Then one of them turned to their silent host.

"And what's your opinion of all this, Rogers? I am sure you are as deeply sorry as we for the persecuted blacks."

Rogers thought a few moments. Then he reached in his pocket, placed a banknote on the table in front of him, and came out with one of the most curtly effective clotures on action-delaying filibuster ever recorded.

"I'm five pounds sorry," he said.

My belief is that it is high time each one of us started deciding how sorry he or she is—in terms of Rogers' bluff-calling interpretation of the word—over the contemporary rape of nature. In this case, however, the currency of sorrow needs to be expressed much more in action and changed attitude than in money. And the thing that ought to make us all feel "rich" enough to pay is the very simple fact that in most places nature is going to be saved not by official bodies but by the community at large. If we don't help, if the whole social climate isn't one of active participation, right down to the personal and household level, then all ordinary wildlife is doomed. The plastic garden, the steel city, the chemical countryside will take over. The government-run parks and national reserves may still survive; but *nature in ordinary life is in the hands of people in ordinary life.*

I still live in a country (England) that has managed to maintain a comparatively healthy relationship with this ordinary nature as distinct from special-preserve nature. And though I certainly don't intend to make a black and white contrast between a holier-than-thou Britain and an unholier-than-I America, I suspect one major difference between the two cultures is in the average person's attitude to the familiar nature around him. In terms of a bad relationship, being sorry means being aware of being wrong. It is an unawareness of being personally wrong (shown both in the negative tendency to blame everything on corporate greed and in certain wrong emphases in current conservation work) that seems to me the weak spot in the United States. This fundamental, personal and private relationship to ordinary nature is primarily what I want to discuss here, and in two or three rather different areas. I hope also to suggest one place, very close to home, where something can be done about the problem.

But first of all I must make one or two painful historical observations.

Why can Britain show a good deal more common wildlife in its cities, towns, suburbs and surrounding countryside than the United States? A great deal of our happier situation is certainly due to completely fortuitous circumstances and not at all to a greater conservation conscience in the British.

American farmers are much more efficient. They change landscapes to suit their machinery. They use more poison. The British farmer has a traditional tolerance toward nature: nine out of 10 are still happy to sacrifice some good farming to some good sport, to provide cover and terrain for game birds, deer, foxes and the rest, and thus cover and terrain for many other species. In any case we have much smaller field systems and they are mostly divided by that best of all natural preserves for small wildlife, the thick hedge. We have also fiercely protected our "common" land, which is traditionally unfarmed and allowed to grow wild. The great landowners of the past have left us an ecologically rich legacy of scattered woodland, and an equally rich legacy of parkland inside town limits. Even without this parkland most British towns have grown so slowly from their medieval origins that they are often much greener and more haphazard than their comparatively instant American counterparts. Nature has never been completely crowded out. In towns and suburbs, too, there are differences in gardening practice (of which more in a moment) that favor our wildlife. But even when all allowance is made for British "luck" in the comparison, there is in my opinion a failing—though much more a passive, historically conditioned failing than an active, conscious one—on the American side.

I was reading recently one of the very first accounts of life in America—Governor Bradford's *Of Plymouth Plantation,* the story of the Pilgrim Fathers' grim early years in Massachusetts. The seeds of the attitude many British nature-lovers still sense in ordinary American life can be seen planted in his narrative. I can best describe it as a resentful hostility to the overwhelming power of the wild land; in Bradford, natural America seems a far worse enemy than the Indians or the machinations and failings of his neighboring colonists. Of course it would be ridiculous to speak of hostility to natural America in the modern United States, but there lingers a kind of generalized suspicion about it—or a cold indifference, as if it may have been officially forgiven the sweat and tears it exacted from the settlers and pioneers, but can't expect to be trusted, let alone loved, for a long time yet—an attitude rather similar to that of many elder fellow countrymen of mine toward the Germans.

To this very old resentment degenerated into indifference must be added later historical factors. Many 19th century European immigrants (such as the Irish and the Italians) came with a bitter Old World experience of depressed and exploiting agricultural economies. One resolve many of them brought with their bags and bundles was a determination never to see farmland again. In sociologists' jargon, the descendants of such immigrants have developed through the years highly urbanized life-styles. Then there is the case of the intellectually dominant subculture of today's America: the Jewish. The one failing that superbly gifted race has (a failing for which they are not to be blamed, since it springs from centuries of being herded into ghettos) is their blindness toward nature. In classical Yiddish, for example, there are very few words for flowers or for wild birds. The great writer Isaac Babel was well aware of this deficiency, which is, sadly, more than I can say for many Jewish friends of my own.

Finally, there is the intensely profit-centered aspect of the American spirit, also to be traced back to the Plymouth Colony days: the drive to maximize the financial utility of any undertaking or resource. You can't set out to rob nature of every cent it has and then still expect it to look flourishing. I admit freely that earlier Americans can be largely excused for their mistaken belief to the contrary. As every historian has pointed out, they were brought up with a sense of endless new territory to be exploited. What did it matter if you ruined the few miles around you when so much still lay virgin? Even today it comes as a shock, so used have we foreigners become to thinking of the United States as one huge polluted conurbation, to see how much wild America still lies between New York and Los Angeles. Every time I fly that route, I find it harder to blame past Americans for their exploiting sins. And it isn't only the size; the image played its part. Naturally the promised land most attracted the poor. Throughout the world the poor have very understandably always been more concerned about making money than protecting the environment. In the past, protectionist action invariably came from a class of society that never went in much for emigration: the well-educated and the well-circumstanced. Safely and comfortably back in Old Europe, they could afford such amenities and fine feelings. The emigrant poor couldn't. But the very obvious irony of our own time is that this characteristic and forgivable poor man's view of nature is still so prevalent in the world's richest nation.

I am not belittling the energy and resources being presently devoted to conservation in the States, but for all that, I suspect that in some ways the approach is still influenced by the old conditioning. Like a certain kind of once unscrupulous millionaire now turned public benefactor, the new official protectionists are overanxious to show off their change of heart, and the problem is being tackled too much in the surely now disproven fashion first tried out on the Indians: that is, in terms of special reservations and salvation showpieces, and not enough in terms of a general re-integration of common nature in ordinary life.

The very word common has a vaguely un-American ring about it. It is the big things, the outstanding things, that call to the virile American heart and pocket. And perhaps this (in many other ways, admirable) national habit of thinking big helps explain why so many urban and suburban environments seem to have been written off by the professional conservationists as hopeless. But these are the environments where most people now live, and where the re-integration is most urgently needed if there is to be any essential ground change in the public attitude. What I believe is required is very simple to say: a will to foster the wildlife, *however insignificant and humble,* in the citizen's own backyard and neighborhood—and *not* to foster the illusion that nature is some large and spectacular rare bird or beast seen on a TV film or glimpsed in a remote national park during a summer vacation.

Where the British score well is at this level. They tolerate the everyday nature round them, because they want it there. They may not be interested in it, but they see it is right that nature should survive and be allowed the conditions to survive. This is something barely conscious; it just seems to us—and with the full implications of that word—natural.

Another wrong (or at least suspect) emphasis in active conservation is that of improving *human* environmental factors, such as atmosphere and water. Very clearly, success there will help other forms of life besides man, and it is not the end result I am questioning but the ruthlessly pragmatic way in which conservation is sometimes presented as a unique need of social man, rather than as a shared need of both man and nature. This can turn the saving of nature into a kind of neutral byproduct of the human concern. I think such an absurdity happens because conservation, though not a uniquely human need, *is* a uniquely human responsibility, and the response of man toward such responsibility has always been *What's in it for me?*

Let me clarify with a simple analogy. I regard what are sometimes called the lower forms of nature as children, and I think we human adults of evolution have precisely the same responsibility toward them as parents toward their own human children. What I dislike in the approach that sells conservation predominantly as a road to the human Pleasant City is that it tends to orphan nature. The protection of the wildlife of the environment becomes like the protection of parentless children: something for specialized agencies and institutions to take care of, not something to concern you or me.

But enough of negative historical deductions. Let's look a little more closely at that fundamental conservation cell: the backyard garden.

I sometimes meet self-styled nature-lovers who say they feed the birds in their garden, they even put up nesting boxes, for God's sake, what more can they do? Then I see their gardens—beautiful gardens, not a weed or a pest in sight among the immaculate lawns and flowers. But what I really see is what isn't there, the total absence of any plant native to the area, the poverty of thick cover (not all birds nest and roost in holes), the ubiquitous evidence of a constant use of insecticides.

What does natural life need? Firstly, it needs privacy, even in the smallest backyard: like humanity, it wants somewhere it can sometimes go and not be seen. Many modern gardens are like glass houses without internal walls, with every function in full view. Secondly, since nature is a self-victimizing process, it needs a supply of victims. You can't massacre all the small nameless insect life of an area and then complain about the lack of butterflies. Plainly these needs call for a change in our whole concept of gardening and gardens. Again, I feel the British are a little ahead of the Americans in this respect—and again for mainly fortuitous, historical reasons.

Apart from anything else, the cultural pressures toward the synthetic garden are much stronger in the United States. There is the high priority put on anything that saves time. Insecticides and weed killers save time. There is the high priority put on good functioning, on neatness and efficiency. Lawns are neat. There is in many suburban areas—and this certainly applies equally to Britain—the high priority put on conforming, on having the same plants, the same layout, though just a little bit better than your neighbors', of course. In America, freedom from crabgrass becomes a test of social acceptability; the man with the best roses walks six inches taller.

In the history of the gardening art the *jardin anglais* has always stood for a profuse disorder. Some American visitors here suppose that the highly formal gardens of some of our Elizabethan and 17th century houses represent the true old English garden. Nothing could be further from the truth, for all these are style-conscious aristocratic copies of Italian and French models. The real English garden has always been first cousin to an English hedge and an English meadow. It has always worked *with* nature, just as the artificial French and Italian styles have worked against (or in spite of) it. And this working with nature is exactly what the ecologically good garden—one honorably shared between the legal human and equally legal natural owners of the place—demands. When a bird or insect flies into town what it looks for from up there is a varied menu and an interesting decor; not one more neon-lit hamburger joint like 50,000 others.

So what should one do?

Obviously the first thing to ban from the gardening shelf is all insecticides, which has been at the start of the nastiest exterminatory chain-reaction in this century. Running it very close is the weed killer. All "scientific" statements as to this or that product's comparative harmlessness can be treated as so much bald-face lying, since they all aim to upset natural balance. The next thing to curtail is the area given up to lawn. Well-kept grass gives a very poor ecological return. Much better is good evergreen cover, especially if it yields in addition nectar-rich flowers and edible fruit or berries. Such cover not only encourages birds but provides an important insect habitat. Another important consideration is the kind of ornamental flower and shrub that is grown. Some of the original species of mints, buddleias, ivies, daisies and the rest may not look as glamorous as their modern "selected" forms, but there is no doubt which the insects find more nutritious.

If you wonder why I keep harping on about insects, the answer is very simple. Before I give it, though, I want to look at another example of the way words can become dangerously obscuring labels. Most insects do fall into that slightly un-American category of mean little indistinguishable things; and just as racialists think all members of the hated race look the same, I am afraid that many Americans bury a major part of the insect universe under the label "bug." There is the symptomatic contemptuous usage "stop bugging me," and all the electronic-mechanical extensions: space bugs, bugged rooms, bugging devices. Under this label all insects tend to become a kind of natural equivalent of the political Reds. Whatever they're up to, it's subversive. Last spring in SPORTS ILLUSTRATED I read of the golfer Frank Beard having combat with this dastardly infiltrator of the American way of life. He wrote: "I had a 30-footer for a birdie, and as I got set to putt a bug lit on my ball, I backed off, shooed it away, lined everything up again, drew my putter back and moved it forward. An instant before impact, the bug flew back on the ball and startled the hell out of me. I left the putt six feet short."

It was with some relief that I read on to find that he didn't actually ask the tournament organizers to call in the spray planes and delouse the whole course at once.

In the circumstances Mr. Beard can be forgiven for feeling about bugs the way the Israelis feel about MIGS: it would be a better game without the damned things. But I quote this passage because what is strange about it to a British reader is this word "bug." We wonder what he really means: a beetle, a fly, a bee, a wasp? It is not only that "bug" in British English is confined to small beetles and their larvae, it is the baffling imprecision and the to us incomprehensible assumption that some forms of life are below the dignity of any American with decently normal drives (both golfing and general) to name.

I have confirmation of this national insect phobia with every American guest I have here in England, as he or she shakes the head over our refusal to install screen doors in our houses. Just when, I can see them asking themselves, will these unhygienic British learn the sanitary facts of life? Well, it may be that more disease-carrying insects are flying about in the United States than with us. But it seems more likely that we make a clearer distinction between the harmless garden and countryside insects that do often fly into the house and those that are a real danger to us. One aid to that distinction is our lack of that blanket word "bug."

And why not bomb the bugs? Because the insect is directly or indirectly the chief food source of countless higher forms of life. If you mercilessly destroy your bugs, you build your conservation house without foundation or a ground floor. You can rate your garden conservationally by checking on the abundance of insect life in it. In this context, if it's clean, it's dirty.

There is really no clearer ethical decision to make in our time: ban the insecticide from your own backyard and get your neighbors to do the same with theirs. But very clearly the process cannot stop there. The vital complement of the conservation garden is some form of local nature reserve. Though I don't doubt the honest intentions of the good people who run many of those I have visited, they seem often to be founded on something of a wrong principle. In fact such local reserves should be known, and their use determined, by a now old-fashioned name for them: nature *sanctuaries*. It is absolutely essential to keep near towns and cities some such unpolluted and wild area open to nature and closed to man; and I'm afraid that being closed to man is not compatible with picnic areas, walk-through paths and similar features installed in the attempt to compromise between social and civic amenity and the true purpose of a wildlife reserve.

But even the conservation garden and its accompanying out-of-town reservoir of wildlife is of little use if all the surrounding farmed country is regularly drenched with insecticide. And here I come to the crux of it. What is urgently needed is rethinking on where conservation is most useful. Instead of thinking of the uninhabited far-off as the ideal area, we ought to reverse the process. Uncontrolled spraying is in any case safest—for humans as well as nature—the farthest possible distance from town; and the town and its wide green belt ought to become the priority conservation zone. This situation has already arisen accidentally in many British towns. Quite a number of once rural species have now taken happily to suburban life in protest against the pollution of their former habitats.

If hedges, small woods and other (from the profit-oriented farmer's point of view) waste areas are to be reinstated in the landscape, it ought to be in just such conservation belts around towns and cities. If the farmers won't listen, then public authorities ought to be made to. Contrary to popular belief, many birds are extremely tolerant of traffic noise. I have even seen them among the scrub on the Los Angeles freeway banks and verges, only a few yards from the steel stream. But one warning: an ecologist must determine the character of the planning. Town-owned free space should be gardened for local nature, not for civic pride and a showy flower display.

I wish there were a way I could lend my own garden here in England instead of trying to say it all in words. I've attempted to practice what I preach. I won't use insecticides out-of-doors. I keep weed killers to the barest minimum. And yes, it is far from being a gardener's dream. About half of it is given over to natural scrub and cover; whatever seeds there happen to be are allowed to grow— thistle, dock, fireweed—no matter how high on the blacklist they figure. It is a town garden, and not very large by American standards. It harbors five or six breeding mammals, a dozen or so species of nesting birds with many more as visitors, a good variety of butterflies and moths and a generally luxuriant insect life. A lot of hard work is saved, since I let nature look after its own part. All I have to do is learn to bear the shocked expressions of the more orthodox gardeners who come round it. I can only report that this social shame is increasingly easy to bear once you have made up your mind to it. You soon realize such people are half blind. They simply don't comprehend the rewards, the richness, the sense of a harmonious creation that such disorder and laziness bring into daily life.

Nothing can annul the prior lien nature has on your property; the title it possessed long before you became the owner, long before you were, even. And there is no argument possible as to where conservation starts. It starts right there, outside your window. That is, it starts if you start, and from the moment you stop merely saying the word conservation in order to avoid its reality. It's no good believing in conservation, agreeing with conservation, talking about conservation. It's one of those words that gives you only two choices. You either do or you damn.

Now let's consider the man with a gun in his hand: the hunter, the prototype of all nature exploiters. Since my views are not going to make me popular, I'd better explain that I'm not, like so many reformers, quite trying to ban the whorehouse. I've always envied the other men but never had the guts to enter myself. I spent a great deal of my youth duck hunting and I can remember very well what it's like some winter dusk when you hear the first swift sough of oncoming wings and see the hit black shape plummet down to splash in the reeds behind you. No other game or sport I've tried has ever given me quite that kick—or made the time wasted on it so endurable.

I was taught to hunt by a man named Brealey, one of the old school. I was not allowed to shoot at a bird until I had proved myself to his satisfaction on the cans and bottles he threw up as a test —and I didn't do that in a day. I was not allowed to shoot at any but legitimate and edible game. I was not allowed to shoot at that unless I could reasonably expect to kill it at the range. I can still recall his code: not above 30 yards with number six shot, above 40 with number four, above 50 with number two. You never, but never, gave up the search for a wounded bird. If night stopped you, you went again the next morning. Only barbarians used automatic shotguns; if you couldn't bring your duck down in two shots (another major crime was "browning"—firing blindly into a pack) that was your fault. You had had your sporting chance. At the time I got irked by all this punctilio. Nowadays, when I occasionally see what we call in this country "town shots" (city people who blaze away at anything that moves) I make silent penance to old Brealey. Like most such men, he was a good field naturalist and a sincere nature-lover as well as being a crisply accurate picker of widgeon and mallard out of a dark sky. He's long dead now, but I think the world hunting community badly lacks men like him as its arbiters.

On one of his "laws" I can't expect to convince Americans—and especially not the gun lobby. Nonetheless I believe the repeating shotgun ought to be banned. Later in life I did use one for a time and it seemed to me not only to make me shoot worse and to wound more than I killed but to take a very essential element out of sport— the sport itself. The thrill of hunting for pleasure is surely killing for pleasure, not just killing at any cost. A two-shot gamble ought to be enough; it's already one more than the golfer has. I have my doubts, in fact, about all the new aids to bigger bags and heavier baskets that the hunting and fishing industries have concocted. All great games depend very strictly on certain agreed limitations and restrictions. The skill lies in beating the system inside the rules. And it is time we started laying down rules on the kind of equipment and behavior hunters and fishermen can and can't be allowed. Both activities are almost purely sports now, and they need to be regulated as sports are.

Another growing necessity is the hunting test. It seems bad enough that a man can buy a gun across the counter without question, but just as bad that he can go straight out and immediately start firing it at any wildlife that crosses his path. I would make a certain standard of marksmanship obligatory before a hunting license was issued; I would ban minors from hunting, for reasons you will guess in a minute; I would also like to see a compulsory course in animal and bird recognition and in general hunting ethics. This is all still a good deal less than what we require of sailors, airline pilots, policemen and other people who hold life and death in their hands.

I gave up hunting myself on the same grounds as many other men: one day I found I couldn't live with the enjoyment I got one moment from seeing birds and animals in the wild and the enjoyment I got the next by killing them. It got harder and harder to pull the trigger. Because you don't just shoot a deer one evening; you also shoot a piece out of every other human being who might have seen and enjoyed the sight of it and its progeny, had it lived. As a kid I shot out of sheer mischief (and well away from my mentor, needless to say) several ravens, even then a rarity in this part of England. Now they are virtually extinct here. I haven't heard that unmistakable deep snoring caw drifting down out of a high blue sky for years. I have to drive to Wales, a hundred miles away, to be sure of hearing it again. What that schoolboy in me helped kill forever—or at any rate, for his lifetime—was one of the last noble and peaceful sounds in his own sky.

Another argument I have very little time for is the one that maintains that hunting helps conservation. Of course, the game the hunter wants to shoot is usually well looked after in terms of bag limitation, closed season and protection of habitat. But everything else suffers, and especially any other wild animal or bird of prey in competition with rifle or shotgun. One of the tragedies of the British conservation story (which, I hasten to add, has many more black spots than you may have gathered from my earlier comparisons) is the abrupt disappearance of many of our once familiar birds of prey over the last 25 years. Insecticides have taken their toll, but a chief enemy remains the professional gamekeeper. Though I loathe their methods—many still use the illegal pole trap and equally illegal poisoned bait—I can't really blame them. They are paid to produce game birds for fall shooting and a full gibbet—the wooden rack on which they hang their "vermin"—proves they have earned their money. It is their bosses who are to blame.

In all so-called conservation for hunting there is a wide streak of tyrannical—almost puritanical—selfishness. No nonhunter would class the sight of a few fat pheasant pecking round a cornfield as more beautiful than a peregrine stooping or a sparrow hawk slashing and tilting its lethal way down a forest clearing. But no neutral person has a say in the matter; the hunting industry decides for us. All this may seem a fairly harmless interference with nature and natural solitude compared with the murderous outpourings of real industry or the scorched-earth techniques of scientific agriculture. But the attitude *is* wrong. It perpetuates, far beyond and outside the psychology of those who do actually hunt, a wrong role of man. It treats nature not as the unfairly threatened and persecuted domain of life it has now become, but as something that is fairly preyed on. It makes killing decent, and killing is never decent. It may be necessary, but not decent. And in America above all it must strengthen the old prejudice—or carelessness—about nature: nature as something hostile, to be hunted down, ultimately down to zero, and driven away from all human settlement. To be used, in a word, at the very time when nature is so clearly asking to be saved for those who come after us.

There are two questions you ought to ask yourself if you do go after nature with a gun. One is this: *Why do I enjoy killing?* The second, and more important, is: *What have I just killed?*

The answer to that second question, let me warn you, can never be just a number and a name. In fact there is only one honest answer in this year of 1970, and only one honest action a hunter can take once he has answered.

If any group seems innocent in the rape of nature, it is that great and amorphous body of amateur natural historians, bird watchers, plant hunters, photographers—nature fans in general. The worst variety of this group, the collector, is happily today a rare specimen himself. One can safely assume that anyone who still collects (*i.e.,* kills) some field of living life just for pleasure and vanity has all the makings of a concentration-camp commandant. Egg collecting, butterfly hunting, taxidermy and all that infamous brood of narcissistic and parasitical hobbies have become so obviously evil that I won't waste time condemning them.

There is, however, a subtler sin for the amateur naturalist that will lead me conveniently to the core of what I want to say about our present defective attitude to nature. I call it identification mania. It is nicely typified by that absurd new game played by some ornithologists: the species-count competition in which on some appointed day bird watchers drive frantically from one locality to the next to see who can accumulate the longest list. And this brings us back very close to the general human fault I started this essay with: our perverse delight in naming things and then forgetting them. If the species count was just the freakish idiocy of a clam-brained ornithological minority, it wouldn't matter. But unfortunately the philosophy behind it contaminates a great deal of our thinking, and our education, about nature.

To a professional scientist correct identification is a basic tool of the trade. But for the non-specialist it seems to me of very secondary importance. Seeing and enjoying nature is infinitely more important than knowing how to name and analyze it. Any trained biologist will tell you that identification expertise has about as much relation to serious biology as knowing national flags has to do with being an authority on international affairs. I put the blame for this narrow and superficial identification approach to nature squarely on the shoulders of the amateur naturalist. Nothing puts the beginner off the whole subject faster than the name-dropping conceit of this kind of expert. The tyro thinks nature must be some kind of academic memory test, a quiz show with no prizes, and quite reasonably takes up something that puts less of a premium on "experience" and know-how (or more accurately, know-what).

Almost all nature education based on the know-what approach is bad, for what goes with it is the notion that everyone ought to get an identification interest in natural history. Of course, if we did all become keen naturalists that would solve all our problems. But if anything is certain about the real situation, it is that many people are never going to be very interested in nature either as science or as a hobby for showing off a cleverness with names. Indeed, as they have less and less contact with nature in our overpopulated world, they are very probably going to be less and less interested in it. What has to be done is to get this vast and growing army of the indifferent to see nature as a daily pleasure of the civilized life. It doesn't have to be named, or studied, or hunted, it just has to be there. And they have to be taught to miss it if it isn't there, the way they would miss electricity or the water supply if that were cut off.

The kind of seeing that this requires is much more esthetic and imaginative than scientific. So for a start I should like to see the scientific element in our school-teaching about nature severely reduced and its place taken by study of the attitudes and vision of the many great painters, poets and writers who have treated the subject. They are who we need most to copy and to learn from, not the scientists. You can always tell the man who wants to experience nature from the one playing at scientist. The former will have granted equality to the whole scene, both in terms of the various families of natural life and in terms of the statistical commonness and rarity of what he is seeing. He won't, in short, be blind to all but his own field. He will know that he has to observe with both the eye of the flea and the eye of the elephant, as the Indian proverb goes. We all see too much with a human eye and to a human scale. He will see the moth's uncurled proboscis and the ancient glacier bed, the smallest and the largest; and all in one glance. He will see forms, colors, structures, see personal, artistic and literary allusions, see whole poetries where the pseudo-scientist sees only names and matter for notes.

One of the curses of our time is that this poetic approach has come to be ridiculed as something rather romantic. It is true that without any scientific check, such an attitude can lead into the turgid bayous of nature-corner sentiment or to the equally nauseating anthropomorphic scripts of the Disney nature films and the kind of commentary one hears at Marineland. If such cheap sentimentality were the only alternative to the scientific approach to nature, I should be all for science. But there is no more need to see nature *either* sentimentally *or* scientifically than there is to see paintings, or listen to music, or enjoy a game or a sport in one of those two fixed manners.

And here, perhaps, there is a stumbling block particular to the American mind, with its inborn pragmatism, its demand for some immediate utility in both the object and its pursuit, and its corollary assumption that the more facts you know about a thing the more there is likely to be in it for you. Europeans enjoy appearances. Americans enjoy things better if they know how they "work"—and of course knowing that involves knowing names. This obsession with labeling and functioning, and the corresponding impatience with the quieter pleasure of mere experiencing, is an aspect of what an American friend of mine once described to me as the single deepest fault of the national culture. He called it a lack of poetry, and then amplified the phrase by saying, "*We try and turn everything into machinery.*" Over the years I have come to see this criticism as a clue to a great deal of what is unhappy in American society.

This is not the place to discuss whether my friend is right in general. But I would choose "unpoetic" as probably the best word to describe the prevailing attitude to natural life in the United States, just as "poetic" best describes the great exceptions to that generalization, the Audubons and the Thoreaus. Poetry, alas, is something you can't sell. All you can do is suggest that it is out there, if people will only find the time and the right frame of mind and discover for themselves that enjoyment does *not* require scientific knowledge.

Myself, I regard nature very largely as therapy. It is where I go to get away from words, from people, from artificial things. It is affection and friendship, too; the recurrence, the return in the cycle of the year of certain flowers, beasts, birds and insects I am fond of. It is sounds. It is curlew on a winter's evening, as I lie in bed. It is the sparrows that chirp on my roof each morning. Above all it is the familiar natural life that lives and breeds round my house—the kind of life any rarity-hunting naturalist would not even notice, it is so ordinary. But I have trained myself, partly through reading about Zen, partly through thinking on the texts of such men as Thoreau, not to take anything in my thousand-times-walked-around garden as familiar. I'm not in the least a religious person, but I suppose the process is something like prayer. You have to work at it. I once told a Benedictine monk that prayer was incomprehensible to me. "Yes," he said, "it was to me once. It becomes comprehensible only through endless repetition."

This, I am convinced, is what practical conservation needs behind it, or beneath it, if it is to work: a constantly repeated awareness of the mysterious other universe of nature in every civilized community. A love, or at least a toleration, of this other universe must reenter the urban experience, must be accepted as the key gauge of a society's humanity, and we must be sure that the re-entry and the acceptance is a matter of personal, not public, responsibility. So much of our communal guilty conscience is taken up by the cruelty of man to man that the crime we are inflicting on nature is forgotten. Fortunately there seem to be many signs in the United States that this "lesser" crime against natural life at last is being recognized for what it is—not the lesser crime at all, but the real source of many things we cite as the major mistakes of recent history. You may think there is very little connection between spraying insecticide over your flower-beds because everyone else in your street does the same and spraying napalm over a Vietnamese village because that's the way war is. But many more things than we know start in our own backyards. Social aggression starts there; and so does social tolerance.

Nature is an inalienable part of human nature. We can never blaspheme against it alone. Exterminate, and you shall be exterminated. Don't care, and one day, perhaps too late, you or your children will be made to care bitterly. Evolution holds no special brief, no elect place for man. Its only favorite is the species that keeps the options open. The nightmare of our century is that so many of man's options are closing on him. A main reason for this is that the individual increasingly lets society and its label-words usurp his own role and responsibility. We all know that we have to get things right between ourselves and the other forms of life on this crowded planet. What we don't, or won't, know is that the getting right cannot be left to government, to the people who are paid to care. I make no apology for saying it again. Conservation can never be someone else caring. It is you caring. Now.

Projects

1. With three or four of your classmates, select a number of poems that provide unique views of nature. Choose some means of organizing your selections. Prepare an introduction for each poem, and then arrange a program in which you orally interpret the poems for your class.

2. Read Stewart Udall's *The Quiet Crisis* (Avon Books, 1967). Report on Udall's documentation of Fowles' opinion that Americans have always felt "a resentful hostility to the overwhelming power of the wild land."

3.   Examine conservationists' efforts in your community or region. Are they resulting in "special reservations and salvation show-pieces" or are they initiating "a general reintegration of common nature in ordinary life"?

4.   Examine the town-owned free space in your city (or on your university or college campus). Is it "gardened for civic pride or showy flower display" or is it maintained with attention to ecological concerns? If possible, interview the persons responsible for planning and maintaining the space. Report their philosophy concerning its purpose and maintenance.

5.   Read *The Firmament of Time* by Loren Eisley (Atheneum Paperback, 1966). Prepare a report discussing Eisley's unique combining of the scientist's and the poet's awareness of the natural world.

Suggested Topics for Writing

1.   Fowles attacks species-count competition as "an absurd new game." Consider the purpose these counts might serve. Defend the action.

2.   Outline means through which we can "get this vast and growing army of the indifferent to see nature as a daily pleasure of the civilized life." Before organizing your remarks, read "Where Life-Style Counts, Who Needs Nature?" by Alan Gussow. Consider the indifferent to whom Gussow refers.

3.   Expand upon Fowles' observation that "conservation gives no choice—you either do or you damn."

4.   Fowles asserts that we must express our concern for the decline of the American environment "more in action and changed attitude than in money." Consider your own actions and attitudes. Have you decreased your demands upon the environment? Rate yourself as a "conservationist." See *Ecotactics: The Sierra Club Handbook for Environment Activists,* particularly "The Activist's Checklist," for a review of action that you might take.

Exercises

1. Study Fowles' introductory paragraphs. What technique has he used to capture your attention? What kind of transition leads from those introductory paragraphs to the body of the essay?

2. Fowles sees in Americans a "failing—though much more a passive, historically conditioned failing than an active, conscious one—" to recognize the value of nature. He finds that Americans have a "very old resentment" toward the natural world "degenerated into indifference." Do you agree? What other essays included in this text have investigated similar attitudes?

3. Summarize what Fowles means by "reintegration of common nature in ordinary life."

4. Fowles' essay is built in part around a comparison of British and American attitudes toward and management of the land. Examine his use of comparison and contrast. How does he organize his remarks? What criteria seem to have determined his selection of details?

5. Fowles observes that "British cities are much greener and more haphazard than their comparatively instant American counterparts." Why does he refer to American cities as "instant"? Is there any way to counter the development of "instant" cities?

6. Fowles discusses the importance of words and the dangers of generalizing through labeling. List other examples of generalizing through labeling.

7. Fowles relates personal experiences in his essay. What is the effect of their use? What proportion of the essay reports personal experience?

8. Examine the diction in the essay. How would you characterize it?

28. *Tualco Valley: Planning a Livable Community*

CLASS PROJECT

For this project, your class and teacher represent the 2000 inhabitants of Tualco Town and the surrounding Tualco Valley. Six square miles of the valley and the surrounding hills, forests, and mountains are represented in the diagrammatic drawing on page 178. The valley is a lovely place now, but it is feeling the pressure of a rapidly growing population. It is your responsibility to plan for orderly development of the valley so that it can accommodate 2000 more inhabitants in the next ten years and yet remain a pleasant community.

For the purposes of the project, divide your class into several groups to represent the various interests of the community:

1. Businessmen of Tualco Town.
2. Homeowners living in the town.
3. Dairy farmers, vegetable, and fruit growers of sections throughout the valley.
4. Frozen food processors whose processing plant is in section 14 and who contract fruit and vegetables grown throughout the valley.
5. Land speculators and developers.
6. Sportsmen.
7. Conservationists.
8. Highway planners and builders.

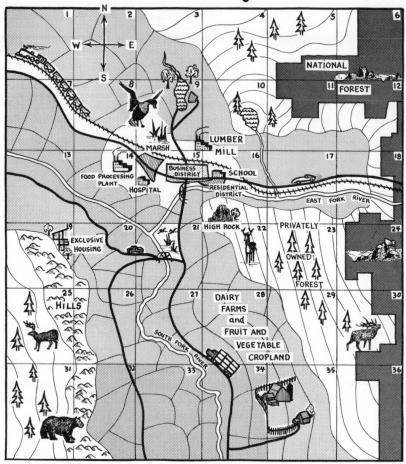

9. Corps of engineers wanting to build a dam on the boundary between sections 17 and 18.

10. Electric power company wanting to run a new power line through the valley.

11. Sanitary district wanting to locate a sewage treatment plant and a sanitary landfill in the district.

12. The mayor and town officials.

13. The urban planning commission.

Select the best location for each of the following developments. Prepare cases for and against controversial locations. Work out compromises. Refer to appropriate articles in this text as you plan your community.

1. A development to accommodate 200 mobile homes.
2. A low-income housing unit to accommodate 25 families.
3. Three moderate-income housing developments to accommodate a total of 75 families.
4. Two large high-rise apartment buildings.
5. A new east-west highway through the valley.
6. A new east-west electrical power transmission line.
7. Expansion in the business district of Tualco Town.
8. A new elementary school.
9. A sanitary landfill.
10. A private resort on one of the lakes north of the town.
11. A sewage disposal unit.
12. A public boat ramp providing access to the river.
13. A convalescent home for the aged.
14. A private duck-hunting range and lodge for hunters.

Also resolve the following land-use controversies which local citizens are already involved in:

1. Whether to build a flood-control dam in sections 17 and 18, creating a large lake and permanently flooding farm and forest land, or to continue to endure damaging floods which occur in sections 13, 14, 20, and 21 about once each seven years.
2. Whether to create a county park at High Rock, a unique rock outcropping, or to permit gravel companies to mine the privately owned rock for use in road building.
3. Whether to extend the National Park into section 23 or to permit clear-cut logging in the area.
4. Whether to permit developers to drain the marsh in the southwest corner of section 9 and build a large shopping center there.

Part Three

THE OUTCOME

29. *Main Street, Smogville*

Vaughn Shoemaker. *Chicago American*. Used by permission.

30. How Come?

DAVID IGNATOW

I'm in New York covered by a layer of soap foam.
The air is dense from the top of skyscrapers
to the sidewalk in every street, avenue
and alley, as far as Babylon on the East,
Dobbs Ferry on the North, Coney Island
on the South and stretching far over
the Atlantic Ocean. I wade
through, breathing by pushing
foam aside. The going is slow,
with just a clearing ahead
by swinging my arms. Others are groping
from all sides, too. We keep moving.
Everything else has happened here
and we've survived: snow storms,
traffic tieups, train breakdowns, bursting
water mains; and now I am writing
with a lump of charcoal stuck between my toes,
switching it from one foot to the other—

this monkey trick learned visiting
with my children at the zoo of a Sunday.
But soap foam filling the air,
the bitter, fatty smell of it . . . How come?
My portable says it extends to San Francisco!
Listen to this, and down to the Mexican border
and as far north as Canada. All the prairies,
the Rocky Mountains, the Great Lakes, Chicago,
the Pacific Coast. No advertising stunt
could do this. The soap has welled out of the ground
says the portable suddenly. The scientists report
the soil saturated. And now what?
We'll have to start climbing for air,
a crowd forming around the Empire State Building
says the portable. God help the many
who will die of soap foam.

31. A Walk on the Towpath

BERTON ROUECHÉ

I was down in Washington around the middle of March, and smelling spring in the air, I gave myself the pleasure of a walk in the country to meet it. The walk I chose was along the towpath of the derelict Chesapeake & Ohio Canal. Situated on the Maryland bank of the Potomac River, the C. & O. Canal extends from the Georgetown section of Washington to a natural passage in the Appalachians at Cumberland, a distance of a hundred and eighty-four miles. The C. & O. is an old canal—one of the oldest lock and mule-drawn-boat canals in the United States. It is also almost the only one of which more than a trace survives. It was begun in 1828, it was completed in 1850, and it remained in operation until shortly after the First World War. The last boats moved through its locks in 1924. It was then stripped of its salvage and abandoned. The depression saved it from piecemeal sale and certain obliteration, and in 1938, through a freak of chance and charity, it was acquired by the federal government. The oldest section of the canal—some twenty wandering miles between the terminus at Georgetown and a point known as Violet's Lock—is now a part of the Washington park system. Its decline has been arrested, and its several locks and lock tenders' houses have all been fully restored. The rest, though reserved as a national monument, has been left to the wild and the weather, and it was there I chose to walk.

I began my walk by car. There is no other ready way to reach the canal once it emerges from the city. A friend with whom I was staying drove me out on his way to work. We passed for a time through an open countryside of rolling pastures and white paddock fences. Then the fences wheeled away and the fields roughened into brush and woods. We came to the head of a rutted lane that wound down the side of a ridge. My friend pulled over and stopped.

"Here you are," he said. "You'll hit the canal just down and around that bend."

I got out. He passed me a lunch that his wife had packed, and a leather-covered flask. I stowed them away in my jacket. "Where am I?" I said.

"Lock 22," he said. "Pennifield's Lock, they call it. Violet's Lock is the next lock up—about three miles from here. Then comes Seneca Creek and Seneca Lock and Aqueduct. That's another mile. After that, it's wilderness all the way to what used to be Edward's Ferry. You won't want to go any farther than that. Edward's Ferry is a good eight miles above Seneca. Maybe more. I'll pick you up there around five." He raised his hand. "Get going," he said, and drove off.

I watched him out of sight, and then headed down the lane. It had rained in the night, and the lane was awash with thin red mud, and puddles stood in the ruts and potholes. It was steep, wet, slippery walking. And cold. Under the trees the morning air had a bite. It felt more like fall than spring. But from what I could see of the sky overhead, the clouds were beginning to break and lift, and there was a hint of a watery sun. I slid down the lane to the foot of the ridge. A coterie of chickadees burst up from a thicket and scattered like a handful of gravel. The lane cut sharply to the left and emerged in a little meadow. At the edge of the meadow stretched the canal. Some fifty feet wide, the color of mud, and flanked by head-high banks, it looked like a sunken road. The towpath followed the farther bank, and beyond it, through a heavy screen of trees, I caught a distant glimpse and murmur of the river. The canal lay as still as a pond. I found a pebble and tossed it in. It sank with a throaty plunk. I guessed the water to be five or six feet deep. About a hundred yards downstream, the canal funneled into a kind of open culvert, which was bridged by a railed catwalk. Facing it, on the towpath side, sat a small white-washed stone house with two stone chimneys and a pitched roof of corrugated iron. That would have been the lock tender's house. The culvert was the lock.

I walked out on the bridge and looked down at the lock. The canal flowed into the lock through a sprung wooden gate just under the bridge. It ran between two narrowly confining walls for about a hundred feet. Then, with a sudden boil and bubble, it broke against another gate, spilled through, and resumed its sluggish course. The walls of the lock were faced with big blocks of rust-red sandstone. Some of the stones were so huge they could have been hoisted into place only with a block and tackle. It was beautiful stone, and it had been beautifully finished and fitted. Time had merely softened it. Here and there along the courses I could even make out the remains of a mason's mark. One device was quite distinct—a double-headed arrow. Another appeared to be two overlapping equilateral triangles. I went on across the bridge to the house. The windows were shuttered and boarded up, and the door was locked. No matter. It was enough just to stand and look at it. It was a lovely house, as beautifully made as the lock, and as firmly designed for function. It gave me a pang to think that there had once been a time when even a lock tender could have so handsome a house. A phoebe called from a sweet-gum tree in the dooryard. Far away, somewhere down by the river, a mourning dove gave an answering sigh. I looked at my watch. It was ten minutes after ten. I started up the towpath.

The sun was still no more than a promise, but the air had lost its chill. It was going to be a spring day after all. The signs of it abounded. Most of the trees that lined the path—sycamore, dogwood, sweet gum, hickory, elm—were coming into bud. Only the oaks still had the wrought-iron look of winter. Some creeping vine— Virginia creeper or honeysuckle—was even in leaf. And everywhere there were birds in sight or sound. Robins hopped and stood and listened at intervals along the way. A woodpecker drummed. A blue jay raced from tree to tree, screaming a wild alarm. There was a flash of cardinal red across the canal. I turned—but too late. It was gone. And so were the lock and the house. They had vanished around a bend. There was nothing behind me but water and woods.

It gave me a curious sensation. I felt for the first time completely alone, but I didn't feel lonely. It was an exhilarating loneliness. It was solitude. I took a deep breath and lighted a cigarette. I felt at peace with the world.

But peace was mine alone. Every step I took spread panic. The sentinel jay was joined by a dozen agitated crows. A terrified rabbit sprang out from behind a fallen tree and ran for its life up the path. I had no choice but to follow it. It erupted again almost under my feet. This time, more sensibly, it took to the woods. I watched it bounding through the brush, changing its course with every bound, and finished my cigarette. I pitched the butt into the canal. There was a tiny splash near the water's edge. I stepped to the bank and looked down and around. Nothing moved but the drifting cigarette. A long minute passed. Then, a foot or two off the opposite shore, the water just perceptibly stirred. The top of a little black head appeared, and then two bright eyes—a muskrat. We exchanged an inscrutable glance. I moved up a step for a better look. The muskrat disappeared without a ripple.

I resumed my walk. Across the canal, the ridge stiffened into a rocky cliff. Pines and cedars grew among the rocks, and the rocks were green with lichen. The canal edged away from the cliff and the river woods thinned out, and the river swept majestically into view. It was high and wide and moving fast. Across the river, beyond a scrubby island, a cloud of gulls hung over the Virginia bluffs. In the slack water at the foot of the island sat a pair of swans. A tremulous whistle recalled me to Maryland. It came from somewhere across the canal, from somewhere up on the cliff, and it sounded something like a redwing. It wasn't a redwing, though. It was a call I had never heard before. I listened, and it came again. It had almost the sound of a blue note. I waited. But the second call was the last. I gave up, and went on. Another phoebe called, and another blue jay screamed another warning. Another woodpecker drummed. The sun began to brighten. And then I heard the river. It was no longer merely a murmur. It was rising into a rumble. The rumble became a roar. That could only mean rapids ahead. A moment later, I saw them—a tumult of dirty white water thrashing down through a rubbly race between the bank and a cluster of islands. But I hardly got more than a glimpse. The path and the river were now a scant twenty feet apart, and the view was abruptly blocked by a levee of earth and rock and hedgerow scrub that rose as high as my head. I walked along the lee of the levee in the enveloping roar of the rapids for almost half a mile. Then, slowly, the roar subsided. It rumbled and grumbled and faded away to a murmur as still as silence. The levee petered out in a tumble of brush, and the river serenely returned. Trees reappeared on its broadening bank and mounted to the edge of the path. I heard a dribble of running water. The towpath took a turn. Just around the turn were a clearing, a footbridge, and a lock—Violet's Lock.

Violet's Lock was a ruin. The sound I had heard was river water flowing into the canal through a silted inlet some yards below the lock. The bridge I had seen was a towpath bridge across the inlet. There was nothing left of Violet's Lock but two walls spanned by a plank. The lock gates were gone, and the lock tender's house had vanished without a trace. I turned away, and saw two fishermen squatting on the riverbank. Both were Negroes and both were wearing shiny windbreaker jackets with Chinese dragons embroidered on the back. One jacket was purple, the other green. The man in the purple jacket gave me a friendly salute.

"What's biting?" I said.

"Man," he said, "don't ask *me* that. I'm just standing here with this line in my hand."

"Cat," the other man said. "I got me one just a little while back." He reached under a bush and held up an eight-inch catfish strung on a willow twig. "It don't amount to much."

"I'm just standing here," the first man said. "I'm just holding this line in my hand."

"Cat's about all you can count on now," the other man said. "Or suckers. But there's carp out there. Big carp. And bass—" He let out a sudden grunt. His line tautened and twitched. He rose to a crouch and gave his rod a jerk. He reeled in a catfish twice the size of the other. "Well, looky there," he said.

"I'm looking, man," the first man said. "That's all I've got to do is just stand here and look."

The other man unhooked the fish, thrust a twig through its gills, and tossed it under the bush. "Cat are funny," he said. "I got that first one on chicken liver. That's what they really like. Some people say that's *all* they like. But this one took a worm. Now I wonder should I try a worm again."

"I'll tell you what I wonder," the first man said. "I wonder how long I'm going to stand here with this line in my hand. I wonder when my turn is going to come."

"No," the other man said. "It's liver they really like. I reckon I'll go back to liver."

I wished them both luck, and moved on.

Above Violet's Lock, the canal was a different canal. It had shrunk to a chain of ponds and puddles, and brush and even sapling trees were growing in its bed. Everything was different. The river broadened until the farther shore was only a haze of horizon. Across the canal, the rocky heights turned into hills and drew half a mile or more away. A stretch of boggy woods appeared, and then patches of marsh alive with caroling peepers. Dandelions bloomed along the path. I passed a clump of what looked like chives. A little farther on was another. Then, suddenly, the clumps were everywhere, swarming up and over the path like day lilies escaped from an abandoned garden. I tore up a clump and sniffed the satin leaves and felt the bulbous root. The leaves had an oniony smell, but the bulb was a cluster of segments. I broke it open, and realized what I had found. The path between Violet's Lock and Seneca Creek was a herbalist's paradise of wild garlic. I pulled up a dozen clumps and put the bulbs in my pocket as a present for my friend and his wife.

It was nearly noon when I reached Seneca Creek. I had thought of Seneca as a possible place to sit down and eat my lunch. One look was enough to change my mind. There was another handsome lock tender's house there. There was a lock and an aqueduct that carried the canal across the creek on three handsome stone arches. There was also a splendid view of the river. That, however, was only part of Seneca. The creek was lined with summer cottages and upended rowboats and real-estate signs and old beer cans and bottles. Off to one side were a big parking lot and a gimcrack summer hotel. The resort was deserted now, but it was easy to imagine in another month or two. I walked past the lock and paused at the aqueduct. Except for the underpinning of arches, it looked much like a lock—a dry and gateless lock. An arrow mason's mark of the sort I had seen at Pennifield's was visible on one of its inner walls, and there were several deep grooves on the sandstone lip of the wall adjoining the path. They had, I supposed, been worn there over the years by the rub of countless towropes.

The peeper marshes and the river woods closed in again. I was back in the cloistered peace of the morning. Beyond the marshes and a screen of trees I caught a glimpse of a low red sandstone bluff. That was probably the source of the stone that built the locks. A downy woodpecker dipped across the canal and into the woods. The woodpecker drumming I had been hearing was probably a downy woodpecker. I all but stepped on a little wood turtle. It crouched under its heraldic carapace with antediluvian patience. I bent down to examine its markings, and there, an inch from its vanished nose, lay a tarnished dime. I pocketed the dime. I picked up the turtle and carried it, with thanks, to its destination on the other side of the path, and continued on my way. The sun burned through the last of the clouds. A glaze of dusty blue spread over the sky, and the muddy canal faded from brown to a mustard yellow. It was almost hot. I began to look for a place to take my nooning.

It required nearly a mile of looking. The edge of the canal was too prickly with brush, and from what I could see of the woods their floor was a jungle of vine-choked seedlings. I finally found what I wanted in a clearing hacked out by a toppled sycamore. It led to the riverbank and an enormous mossy boulder. Near the boulder was a greening willow tree with a cascade of branches trailing out into the water. I sat down in the dappled shade of the willow and leaned back against the boulder. I was tired. For a moment, I simply sat there. I hadn't known how tired I was. But I was also limp with hunger. I got out the lunch that my friend's wife had prepared, and opened the pocket flask. I sniffed and felt better and took a swallow. It was wine—*rosé.* I unpacked my lunch. She had given me a roast-beef sandwich, a Swiss-cheese sandwich, a fried chicken leg, and a hard-boiled egg. The egg was still in its shell, and on the shell she had drawn a grinning pumpkin face. It seemed a shame to immediately shatter so nice a surprise. I put the egg aside and ate the sandwiches and the chicken leg, and washed them down with the wine. But I was still hungry. I cracked the egg and ate it with a pinch of salt and pepper that I found in a twist of foil. I lighted a cigarette and finished off the wine, and watched the river roll by.

My eye was caught by a duck in the water. It sat drifting along on the current just offshore, and I recognized it as a diving duck—a tiny bufflehead. The bufflehead is one of the smallest and loveliest of ducks, but it wasn't its beauty that caught and held my eye. It was its posture. Its body was headed upstream; it was coming down tail-first. I watched it with astonishment, and then with a kind of alarm.

It was floating straight for the trap of trailing willow branches. Another few feet, a few more seconds, and it would be in among them. I waited for it to dive or change its course. But it seemed entirely oblivious. It sailed brainlessly into the trap. A branch touched its back. It swung around, gave a petulant squeak, and dived. A moment passed. I scanned the water above, beyond, and below the willow. There was a squeak from under the tree. The duck was back exactly where it had been before. It submerged again. This time, it came up in open water, but its situation was not much improved. It was upstream of the tree once more, and only just clear of the branches. The touch of a branch sent it into another dive. It was down for what seemed like a minute. And this time it surfaced in safety—well beyond the willow and several feet below it. It turned slowly around a time or two. Then, fixing its gaze on some distant point upriver, it let the current take it. It sailed away, and out of sight, tailfirst.

I stood up and stretched. It was time to go. My watch said twenty minutes to two, and I still had a walk of six or seven miles ahead of me. I dug a hole and buried my litter and walked back through the clearing to the towpath. The peepers were still peeping in the marsh. A big fox sparrow ducked out of sight in a thicket. The character of the woods began to change. They had an older, darker, more primitive look, and most of the trees were festooned with monstrous grapevines. They looped and drooped and hung over the path like inextricably tangled ropes. Many of the vines were as thick as my wrist. Some were the size of my ankle. I caught hold of one that dangled from a branch near the edge of the canal and was tempted beyond my age. I gave it a tug. It would easily bear my weight. I got a good grip and moved back a few steps. There was nobody looking. I took a run and a jump, and swung into the air— over the path, over the bank, out over a patch of canal. And back. I let go, stumbled, and landed hard on my rump. I climbed to my feet. I seemed to be all right. No broken bones. No bruises. No harm done. I brushed myself off and moved briskly on up the path. I wasn't even out of breath. I was only out of countenance.

A tremulous whistle sounded overhead. It was the blue-note bird again. I stopped dead in my tracks and peered cautiously up through the trees. Another whistle. Something moved, or seemed to move, high up in a twisted hickory, but I was looking into the sun, and it could have been anything—a branch, a vine, a shifting shadow. I waited in a vacuum of silence. Another movement, another call, and I might be able to place it. The silence broke in a thump of approaching hoofs. Well, that took care of that. I shrugged, and moved on. Two girls on horseback came trotting into view down the path. They were riding abreast, but at the sight of me they reined up, and one dropped back. The lead rider was an easy, smiling, golden girl in jodhpurs and a lavender turtleneck sweater. She smiled and waved. I backed off the path.

"Hi there," she said, and stepped her horse neatly past me.

Her companion wore blue jeans and sneakers. She was dark and grim and hanging on for dear life. She gave me a hurried glance.

"Don't kick now," she said to her horse. "Please don't kick."

I shrank farther into the brush that lined the bank. The golden girl waited for her companion to lurch abreast, then touched her horse back to a trot. They jogged out of sight toward Seneca, and I continued on my way. The marks of their passage were all over the path. At one point, the track was scarred in a wild and ragged circle, and there were several hoofprints precariously close to the brink of the canal. It could have been an awkward drop. The canal was no longer a trickle of ponds and puddles. It was wider and deeper and looked almost like a canal again. Before long, I thought I saw why. The marsh rose into a scrubby field, and at the foot of the field it drained into a little brook. But I was mistaken. I should have known that the canal had been better engineered than that. The brook didn't flow into the canal. It flowed under it and on to the river through a culvert. There must be another inlet at Edward's Ferry or beyond. I heard a crash of wings and a bedlam of squeaks and squawks, and a dozen wood duck exploded from the water. They beat up the canal, just skimming the surface, and wheeled sharply into the woods. Across the canal, the scrub thickened and then was choked abruptly off at a barbed-wire fence. Beyond the fence was a pasture that stretched ahead as far as I could see. A green-and-white striped horse van stood tilted under a big elm near the canal, and in the distance, on the slope of the ridge, stood a broad white house with a façade of six white columns. It looked as if I had emerged from the wild.

I had. After about a mile, the pasture rolled away behind a sycamore grove, and the canal swung back toward the river. Through the trees up ahead I could see the rusty roof and double chimneys of a lock tender's house. Then the river woods opened into a clearing, and a shantytown of shacks and sheds and broken-down trailers mounted on cement blocks appeared. One of the trailers had a wooden sign nailed over the door: CAMP FUN. A man in a blue yachting cap and a sweatshirt was sitting on the doorstep. He stood up when he saw me, and stared. He shambled across the yard, still staring. At the same moment, a little brown dog with a terrier face and the tail of a collie came yapping around the trailer. The man turned.

"Shut up," he said, and gave the dog a kick in the ribs.

The dog sat down. It opened its mouth and yawned. The man came up to the edge of the path.

"Nice day," he said.

"Yes," I said. "Very nice."

"You live around here?" he said.

"No," I said. "I'm just taking a walk along the canal."

"Is that right?" He leaned against a tree. "I live up at Poolesville. But I got me this camp down here at the Ferry."

I looked at my watch. It was almost five o'clock. "Well," I said, and turned to go.

A blue-note whistle came from across the canal. I turned back.

"Did you hear that?" I said. "That whistle?"

"Sure," he said. "What about it?"

"What is it?" I said.

"That?" he said. He looked at me, and shrugged. "Some bird, I reckon."

Projects

1.   Read Roueché's entire book, *What's Left: Reports on a Diminishing America.* Write a paper summarizing Roueché's experiences and his concerns.

Suggested Topics for Writing

1.   Recall a time when you recognized the beauty of a particular natural area, the ugliness of a once-lovely area, the impressive architecture of a building. Or recall a situation in which you recognized the value of some aspect of your physical environment you had previously taken for granted. Write a personal experience paper in

which you recreate your experience in a manner that will enable others to share it.

Exercises

1. Roueché recounts a day spent on the towpath of the Chesapeake and Ohio Canal. Notice the interplay of description, dialogue, and anecdote. What purpose does each serve?

2. Study one of the descriptive passages in the essay, particularly observing Roueché's careful use of transition to locate the item he describes.

3. Roueché makes effective use of descriptive verbs. List the verbs from a single paragraph. Which are active? Which are passive? Which are highly descriptive? Discuss the value of effective verbs.

4. What is the purpose of the capsule history with which Roueché opens his essay?

5. After describing the lock tender's house at Pennifield's Lock, Roueché writes, "It gave me a pang to think that there had once been a time when even a lock tender could have so handsome a house." Why can a lock tender no longer "have so handsome a house"?

6. Consider Roueché's vocabulary. Define *aqueduct, coterie* of chickadees, *throaty* plunk, *inscrutable* glance, *tremulous, rubbly race, scant, caroling peepers, gimcrack* summer hotel, *heraldic carapace,* and *antediluvian.* Is Roueché's diction formal, informal, or a combination of both?

7. What is the effect of giving the particular names of birds, trees, and flowers, instead of merely referring to them by general names?

8. After describing his meeting with the girls on horseback, Roueché comments, "The marks of their passage were all over the path." Did Roueché leave any marks of his own passage? What about the cigarette butt that he pitched into the canal, the garbage he buried, and the garlic he dug? What are the long-range effects of such actions, particularly in frequently visited areas?

9. Of what significance is Roueché's conversation with the man who owns "Fun Camp"?

10. What is Roueché's purpose in the essay? How is his conversation at "Fun Camp" related to his purpose?

11. Fowles, in his essay "Bugs, Weeds, Americans," argues that we are overconcerned with "naming" of birds. Did Roueché merely want to name the bird whose song he heard?

32. Catastrophe by the Numbers

CHARLTON OGBURN, JR.

The poet, who a century and a quarter ago, "dipt into the future, far as human eye could see" and "saw the Vision of the world, and all the wonder that would be," would, if he dipt into it today, find disaster for the human race squarely ahead down the road our species is travelling with gathering speed. Even in 1842, however, when Tennyson's paean of optimism and affirmation was published, there was no need to have been unprepared for the fate mankind now appears bent on bringing on itself. More than forty years earlier, the professor of history and political economy at East India College in Hailey-bury, England, the Reverend Thomas Malthus, had called attention to the fact that the power of the human race to reproduce itself is infinite, while the capacity of the earth to support its numbers is finite. By 1842 birth rates and death rates in England, which had been in a rough balance a century before, showed a wide disparity. Owing to a fall in the death rate, the annual excess of births over deaths had reached thirteen per thousand persons, which meant that in another fifty years the population would double.

Death rates for the human race as a whole have been tumbling ever since, as science has been bringing the big killers of mankind under control and extending its beneficent sway from the advanced parts of the world to the less favored. The paradoxical result has been that human existence is threatened. Scientists concerned with the world's future have for a decade and more been urging mankind to grasp and be guided by the ominous statistics—so far with little response. The figures cannot be too often rehearsed.

The population of the world, from an estimated five million 8,000 years ago, reached 500 million about 300 years ago, having doubled about every 1,000 years. It reached one billion before 1850, having doubled in less than 200 years. Two billion was reached about 1930—the doubling period having been reduced to about eighty years. The population of the world is now over 3.5 billion, and the doubling period is now down to about thirty-five years. *Every day* the population goes up by 190,000—the equivalent of a fair-sized city.

The joker in the population pack—the terrible, cruel joker—is that with a rate of population increase that is constant, or even somewhat declining, the population will not only continue to grow, but the amount by which it grows will *every year become greater*. The principle is that of compound interest. If the present rate of population increase were to continue, at the end of only 650 years there would be one person for every square foot of the earth's surface. Such a horror could not, of course, actually come to pass. If birth rates had not long since been sufficiently reduced to bring them back into balance with death rates, nature would have achieved the same end by scourging mankind with one of the traditional mass killers—war, famine, and plague—or with a more modern agent, crippling psychic ills.

The rate of population increase is highest in the poorer countries. What most of us have failed to grasp, however, is that the rate of increase is menacing in the United States—menacing to ourselves and, because of our disproportionate demands on the world environment, menacing to everyone else. As in other technologically advanced countries, though less so than in some others, the birth rate in the United States has markedly declined in the past century. Nevertheless, our population, having passed 100 million in 1917, passed 200 million in 1967. Even at the present low fertility rate (the birth rate for women of childbearing age), which is the lowest since the 1930's, it will reach 400 million before a child born today is seventy years old (by which time the population of the world will have reached fifteen billion). When the Republic is as old again as it is now, in 2162, the number of Americans will be getting on toward 1.5 billion, while many children born that year may live to see the equivalent of the entire population of the world today jammed into the United States.

To picture what is in store for us as the population mounts we do not have to peer into the future far as human eye can see. We need only apply a little imagination to the effects of population pressure that we are already enduring. Nearly all of the problems we are wrestling with today are being rendered far more difficult of solution by the addition of nearly 5,500 lodgers to the national boardinghouse every day—such problems as providing adequate education and job training, housing, medical services, parks, playgrounds, sports fields and swimming pools, highways, airports and rapid mass-transit, and the wherewithal to relieve the plight of the poor in slums and rural backwaters. If we are finding urban problems today almost more than we can manage, how are we going to handle them as the cities are swelled by ever more millions? Our streams and lakes are already so befouled with human, industrial, and agricultural wastes that to clean them up will cost one hundred billion dollars, we are told. Our garbage is piling up around us: a million tons more every day, according to specialists at the Massachusetts Institute of Technology. Noise, taking a toll in health and efficiency and generally adding to the strain of life, has been doubling in volume every ten years. The cost of maintaining a nation of 200 million in the ever more expansive style to which we are accustomed comes high, and it bears not on the American people alone. With one seventeenth of the world's population, we consume two fifths of its production of raw materials, and, even with allowance made for the finished products we return, the disparity is enormous. Into the common atmosphere of the earth we Americans annually pour 140 million tons of pollutants, of which some ninety million come from transport (we burn more gasoline in motorcars than the rest of the world put together) and more than fifteen million from electric power generation (of which our share of the world's total is a third). Our contribution to the carbon-dioxide content of the atmosphere, which has gone up by over 10 per cent in the past century (and which by creating a "greenhouse effect" could result in the melting of the polar ice caps and the inundation of all the world's ports and coastal plains) is comparable to our share of the world's fossil fuel combustion—34 per cent.

Within thirty or thirty-five years we may expect to have 100 million more Americans generating refuse, water pollutants, and toxic gases; demanding their share of the world's resources and of our own—forests and minerals, soil and water. We shall have the same 100 million more taxing those services which already the nation is supplying with difficulty—where, indeed, it is not already woefully in arrears. As the population continues to soar, the costs of providing for its needs will far outpace it. For example, to supply water-deficient areas of the western part of the continent there is already being proposed a North American Water and Power Alliance to redirect southward the flow of several large Canadian rivers now emptying in the north—at a price of one hundred billion dollars: just to have water come out of the faucets.

And that will be only part of it. The inflation of any commodity results in its devaluation, and so must it be with human life. Humanity, from having been an object to be loved and cherished, will become one to be escaped, which will scarcely be possible as the teeming hordes press in on the resorts of privacy, convert the cities into the psychological equivalent of concentration camps, and necessitate a regimentation and computerization of life in order to manage the packed masses. Human inflation must also strike at the individual's estimate of his importance. The average American, from having been one hundredth or one thousandth part of a rural community or town two centuries ago, has become one two-hundred-thousandth part of a city today; if he is on the young side of middle age, he can expect to be reduced to one thirty-millionth part of a megalopolis. As the individual is overwhelmed by and lost in a society of ever more monstrous and inhuman forms, we must anticipate a progressive multiplication of the symptoms of anomie and alienation, which range from apathy and despondency to aggression and violence.

We shall also witness the desolation of what remains of the natural world around us and the closing of avenues of escape from the mounting tensions of an increasingly overwrought, high-pressure civilization. Beaches, lakes, mountains—the green kingdoms that have always stood for the living world in our eyes and have been the matrix of every human culture—will be overrun, debased, and obliterated by the products of that civilization, human and material. The process accelerates rapidly today. The cottages crowd rank on rank along the shores and lakesides. The suburbs spread like a skin eruption ever farther into farm land, and with them come the shopping centers and industrial plants, converting fields and forests to asphalt, masonry, and neon lights in eighty- and hundred-acre swoops. To the rear, even as they spread outward, the cities are cut to pieces by freeways on which, beneath thickening palls of smog, swelling streams of motorcars race eight abreast.

Of course, events in the world at large may preclude the climax of this spoilage. Despite our poor, the average American can purchase nine times as much in the way of goods and services as the average Latin American, and more than twenty times as much as the average Asian or African. And the have-not peoples are ill content with this dispensation. There has been let loose in the world a so-called "revolution of rising expectations." Actually, those expectations only *aim* at revolution. They amount to a demand, affecting billions, for the health and comforts the West has shown to be attainable. We might ask ourselves what course those billions are likely to take as they see the disparity between what they have and what we have grow wider—as it is doing—and if they see no prospect of substantial relief from their poverty under the institutions they are accustomed to. At the same time we might ask ourselves what the consequences would be if their expectations of the more abundant life were met: what overwhelming demands would be made on the resources of the globe, and what damage done to the environment of life if the incomes of the disadvantaged billions should approach our own and all peoples began to live on the American model—felling forests for paper as we do, burning fuels and pouring pollutants into the air and the rivers and the sea as we do, and consuming an equivalent share of the earth's minerals. "The ecology of the earth," says Harvard nutritional expert Jean Mayer, "—its streams, woods, animals—can accommodate itself better to a rising *poor* population than to a rising *rich* population."

What remains clear is that the higher the rate of population growth among the economically laggard peoples—and, to repeat, it is now the highest in the world—the slower any improvement in their lot is likely to be, and the more costly to the earth and its ecology would be the dramatic improvement we have taught them to expect. Year by year the alternatives ahead grow more dangerous. With a continuation of present rates of world population growth, either progress or lack of progress in satisfying the wants of the multiplying billions will alike become ever more hazardous, ever more certain to be destructive of world order.

How vast a human multitude the planet can feed is moot. Fanatic agriculturalists speak of 50 billion and more and present us a graphic picture of the world's forests being "sheared off at ground level" by "a huge steel blade . . . pushed by a heavy crawler-type tractor" to provide farm land. That forests are indispensable in preserving watersheds and water tables and tempering climates, that the need will be for more forests in the future to provide lumber and pulp, does not seem to concern them. But at least they point up the insanity of devoting our energies, not to creating conditions in which man's potentialities may be realized, but to converting this splendid earth into a dreary food-factory to provide a mere subsistence for overflowing billions with whom no one in his right mind could wish to see the planet burdened.

The nightmare that the population explosion has in store for their descendants has been persistently pictured for the American people. Congress, no longer palsied before native obscurantism or the medieval theology of the Vatican, has—admirably—appropriated substantial funds for research into human reproduction and for the dissemination of information on contraceptive techniques. Yet the public on the whole continues to show itself passively or actively on the side of catastrophe—not on the side of its prevention.

In the face of all warnings, we Americans brought over 3.5 million new human beings into the world last year, to send the population of the United States up by 1.5 million. And with each of these added lives representing a burden on the earth equal to a half dozen or more Asians or Africans, we should perhaps not expect those unenlightened folk to be much moved by our exhortations to them to reproduce less. A Gallup poll in November a year ago showed that 41 per cent of Americans considered *four or more* children ideal for a family, the percentage being 50 among Roman Catholics, 56 among Negroes, and higher than average among the poor—47.

Admittedly, there were once good reasons for large families. At the time of the American Revolution, only half of the children born lived to sixteen. Most of us were farmers, and on the farm children were an asset. In any case, land and resources appeared inexhaustible. Let it be acknowledged too that while times have changed drastically, asking couples to limit the number of their children is asking a great deal. Watching a human personality gradually take shape, one that you have helped bring out of nothing, is an incomparable satisfaction. Children lend a kind of charm to life that nothing else can.

That the traditional indulgent view of large families should die hard is not surprising. The fact remains—and it is a fact of which there is no excuse for ignorance—that those who reproduce as if they were living in the past are preparing for the children of the future a world in which life will scarcely be worth living. Yet evidently little stigma attaches to their doing so. If suburban mothers hesitate to traipse across the shopping center with a train of offspring, nothing in their bearing betrays it. A father of ten grins with self-satisfaction out of the television tube on "Generation Gap," while another parent beside him apologizes for being, by comparison, an underachiever. A prominent clergyman of the nation's capital and his wife are evidently unembarrassed at having brought nine children into the world. Newspapers regularly report the plight—and complaints—of parents of twelve on relief, without any suggestion that society has rights in the matter, rights which have been grossly violated. Public figures who have become known partly because of their concern with the nation's future, like columnist Jack Anderson and entertainer Dick Gregory, can have nine and seven children, respectively, and not feel that they owe the public an apology any more than John Wayne, who also has seven children. The governor of New Jersey, Richard J. Hughes, had three children by one wife, acquired three more with a second wife, and by her had an additional three. Presumably his career has not been impaired as a result—or Governor Nelson Rockefeller's by his having six children, or ex-Congressman Hugh L. Carey's by his having had fourteen.

The crucial test of public opinion on the issue came last year when a strong bid for the presidential nomination was made by a dynamic and appealing young politician whose ten children (with an eleventh on the way) marked him as entirely disqualified to address himself to the problem that Dwight Eisenhower had called one of the most critical of our time. During his campaign for a Senate seat Robert Kennedy had indeed light-heartedly confessed to this disqualification. The next year he had gone further. Speaking in a country in which one of the world's most rapidly growing populations had for two decades been outstripping an already inadequate food production by 10 per cent—Peru—he gaily challenged his audience to outbreed him. ("Deadly dangerous," the Washington *Post* termed the ploy, and with reason. If all the speaker's eleven children and their descendants reproduced as he had, there would be over 214 million descendants of the Robert Kennedys in the ninth generation, and seven times as many as there are people in the entire world today in the eleventh.) Not only, however, did Senator Kennedy's exemplification of the procreative irresponsibility that is pushing the world toward catastrophe create no bar to his political ambitions; no public figure, editorialist, or columnist that I know of deemed it important enough to mention as bearing on his eligibility for the supreme office.

In a statement hailed by family-planning groups, the heads of thirty governments in the United Nations have announced "that the opportunity to decide the number and spacing of children is a basic human right." Not to *limit* but to *decide* the number. What this "right" is, of course, is the "right" of any part of the human race to make the planet uninhabitable for the whole. It is the "right" of any passenger in a lifeboat to help himself to as much of the provisions as he wants, regardless of the consequences to his fellows.

Just as early humanoids were probably unaware of any connection between sexual intercourse and its subsequent issue, so their descendants today, one could almost believe, are unaware of any between the number of children individual couples have and the growth of the population as a whole. That would explain how the *Reader's Digest* can run an excellent article hammering home the implications of the problem, and in an advertisement a few months later, beam upon John and Mary Ann Forristal of Houston and their nine children as a representative *Digest* family. It would explain the report issued in November, 1968, by a committee of highly qualified citizens set up by the President to recommend steps to deal with population pressure. On one page the report tells us that the current rate of growth of the American population "cannot be maintained indefinitely," on the opposite that the national objective is "a society in which all parents can have the number of children they want and when they want them." What we do if the number of children parents want must produce a rate of population growth impossible to maintain, which is the case at present, the committee does not say. Last July, in the strongest public statement on population yet made by an American President, Mr. Nixon detailed the enormous scope of the problem and proposed the creation by Congress of a "Commission on Population Growth and the American Future"; then he went on to vitiate all he had been urging with the pious pronouncement that the government's pursuit of the goal of population control would "in no circumstances . . . be allowed to infringe upon the religious convictions or personal wishes and freedom of any individual, nor . . . to impair the absolute right of all individuals to have such matters of conscience respected by public authorities." One wonders how close to final debacle we shall have to come before a President summons up the nerve to do what is clearly imperative now and gives the American people to understand that if they care anything for posterity, for their country, and for the handiwork of the Creator that has made North America so hospitable and inspiring to human habitation, they are going to have to accept a ceiling on the number of children per couple, and that the national interest will be best served if that ceiling for the present is no more than two.

Even if such a national policy were enunciated, however—as sooner or later it will have to be—there will remain the question of how individual couples are to be brought to conform to it. What results could be expected from a mere appeal to conscience?

Harmful ones, Garrett Hardin of the University of California argues persuasively. The person whose conscience is appealed to, says Professor Hardin, is caught in a "double bind" of a kind that can induce schizophrenia. For he is damned if he does and damned if he doesn't. If he ignores the appeal and has three or four children, he stands to be publicly condemned as selfish, irresponsible, and antisocial. If he obeys it while others ignore it, he can only feel he has been had—one whom others "secretly condemn . . . for a simpleton."

Of course, we should not have to fear these consequences if an appeal to conscience were *uniformly* acceded to. But one thing that experience of this world should teach us is the futility of expecting human beings in the aggregate to curb their instincts or desires for any length of time just for the general good. Were it otherwise, we could have government by exhortation instead of by laws—laws with teeth in them. Can it be imagined that wartime rationing that depended on voluntary compliance would be of any effect? And rationing is what we are talking about.

To move human beings to what is uncongenial and unnatural to them requires the carrot and/or the stick. For the great majority of us, over the long run, nothing else will serve. The question is, what sort of carrot and what sort of stick would be most likely to prove effective in preventing the earth from being swamped by people and at the same time provide an equitable apportionment of the right to bear children? That is the question to which those most concerned with the future of life on earth should address themselves—or show how these ends may otherwise be achieved.

Professor Hardin favors coercion—but "mutual coercion, mutually agreed upon by the majority of the people affected." Social sanctions could perhaps meet the need. If anyone with three or four children automatically brought obloquy and ostracism on himself as an antipatriot and an offender against the Deity (who presumably would have some interest in the preservation of his magnificent creation, the earth), we might have the answer. But the world might be close to irreversible disaster, or over the line, before such an effective consensus could form, even in the United States.

Meanwhile, economic levers are available. Federal and state income-tax exemptions now authorized for every minor child could be denied in the case of children over the number of two, born nine months or more after the enactment of the legislation. Annual payments could be made to sexually mature females who refrain from bearing children, and in lesser amounts to those who stop with two. Fines, proportionate to the offender's capacity to pay, could be levied against parents for each child they produce in excess of two; beyond a certain limit the offenders could be deprived of the right to vote. (Why should those indifferent to society's future be given a voice in it?) At the same time, of course, anti-abortion laws—which in any case represent a tyrannical denial by the state of the rights of an individual—should be repealed; contraceptives should be made freely available to all, and every effort should be made to devise simpler, surer, safer methods of contraception.

Obviously, strong opposition to any program equal to arresting the population explosion is to be expected, especially on the part of the Roman Catholic hierarchy. But public opinion can be swayed. The Vatican has changed its mind in the past, and can and must change it again. The more public discussion there is, the sooner the public will become accustomed to and will accept measures to deal effectively with a crisis that four thousand scientists at a recent meeting of the American Association for the Advancement of Science termed—along with the related crisis of pollution—the most serious facing mankind. Too-long delay in meeting it can result only in having the issue taken out of our hands, for under the strains to which the population explosion must increasingly subject civilization, the institutions of representative self-government will be among the surest to give way.

Projects

1.   Reconsider "Tualco Valley: Planning a Livable Community." What kinds of changes would result if the population of the valley were to double? Which would have negative effects on the area? Which positive?

2.   Ogburn warns that continuing population growth will result in the desolation of what remains of the natural world. Yosemite National Park in California is already feeling the impact of our growing population. Research the problems resulting from heavy use of the park. What measures have been taken to deal with the problems?

3.   Investigate the development of synthetic foods. Do they offer a solution to the food needs of a continually growing population? Consider the aesthetic factors such as taste, the satisfactions of chewing (for example, carrot and celery sticks), the pleasure of smelling food cooking, and the appearance of what one is about to eat, as pleasing side effects of contemporary food which human beings might wish to retain.

4.   Examine our "traditionally indulgent view of large families" as it is evidenced in advertisements. Survey several 1960s issues of popular magazines. Then survey current issues of the same magazines. Are families with more than two children pictured in current advertisements as frequently as they were in the 1960s?

5.   Recently advertisements supporting population control have appeared in magazines. Examine several advertisements. Discuss the kinds of appeals they contain. Do you believe the advertisements will have a positive effect?

Suggested Topics for Writing

1.   Ogburn asserts that by producing too many children we are preparing them for a life hardly worth living. Envision life in an

overpopulated city in the year 2075. Prepare a one-act play drama-
tizing some aspect of life as it might be in 2075.

2.   Discuss your own reaction to suggestions that family size be
regulated by law. Particularly consider the conflict between *intellectual appreciation* of the need for controlling population growth
and *emotional reaction* to legislative interference in private decisions.
How can this conflict be resolved?

3.   Malthus long ago warned that human population was outgrow-
ing earth's capacity to support it. Will the present warnings, like
Malthus', also produce no results? Why or why not?

Exercises

1.   How convincing is Ogburn's essay? What kinds of evidence
support his thesis that the world is facing a population crisis?

2.   What techniques has Ogburn used to make population statistics meaningful?

3.   Ogburn frequently uses figurative language. What are some
examples? What is the effect of their use?

4.   Summarize the reasons why the population of the United States
makes a disproportionate demand on the world environment. What
changes in your life-style would be necessary to reduce these demands?

5.   Ogburn believes that overpopulation results in "human inflation" and "devaluation." Do you agree?

6.   List Ogburn's proposals for curbing population growth. What
are the weaknesses of each proposal? Suggest other means of regulating population growth.

33. Man Overadapting

RENÉ DUBOS

Until the past few decades, most technological and social changes were gradual and affected only a small percentage of the population at any given time. The rate of change was slow enough for man to adapt—the physiological and anatomical characteristics of his body underwent alterations to fit the new circumstances, and so did his mental attitudes and social structures.

But now the environment is changing so rapidly that the processes of biological, mental and social adaptation cannot keep pace. A tragedy of modern life is that the experience of the father is of little use to his children.

Hazards

As everyone knows, man's life expectancy at birth has greatly increased during recent decades, especially in affluent groups. This has been due almost entirely to a reduction in infant mortality. People do not live significantly longer than they used to, but medical advances have allowed more of them to make it through nutritional and microbial hazards of infancy.

Although life expectancy at birth has increased, the expectancy of life past the age of 45 has not changed significantly, if at all. Modern adults do not live longer than their counterparts at the beginning of the Century. Even with affluence and modern medical care, they are still disease-ridden. Cardiac conditions, cerebral strokes, various types of cancers, arthritis, emphysema, bronchitis, and mental afflictions are among the many chronic ailments that plague all affluent technological societies—they are the diseases of civilization.

Response

Death by these diseases is not due to lack of medical care. In the United States, for example, scientists and especially physicians have shorter life expectancies than members of other social groups even though they belong to privileged social classes that have ready access to medical attention.

The simple fact is that we know very little about most chronic and degenerative diseases. We do know, however, that they are not inherent in man's nature, but are caused by environmental and social influences that are ubiquitous in the technological world. They are the expressions of man's failure to respond successfully to modern ways of life.

An analogy may be seen in the first phase of the Industrial Revolution during the 18th Century. Many of the workers had come recently from agricultural areas. They found it difficult to adapt to the appalling conditions in the cities, and there was a profound deterioration in their physical and mental health. Later, through a multiplicity of medical and social measures, men were able to adapt to the health threats associated with the factories and tenements in mushrooming industrial cities. But new health problems arise from any sudden and profound disturbance in man's way of life.

Balance

Clearly our adaptive potentialities are not unlimited. Even now they may be exceeded by some of the stresses created by contemporary technological developments. In the course of his prehistoric evolution, man was repeatedly exposed to seasonal famine, inclement weather, infectious processes, physical fatigue, and many forms of fear. This evolutionary experience has generated in his genetic constitution the potentiality to adapt to many different kinds of stresses. But he now faces dangers that have no precedent in his evolutionary past. He probably does not possess the responses that will be necessary to adapt to many of the new environmental threats created by modern technology: the toxic effects of chemical pollutants and synthetic substances, the physiological and mental aberrations resulting from the mechanizations of life, the artificial and violent stimuli that are ubiquitous in the technological world.

Rhythm

Modern life is almost completely divorced from the cosmic cycles under which man evolved and to which his constitution is intimately geared. Every person shifted from day to night duty or vice versa is aware of the mental and physical difficulties that result from disturbances in his hormonal rhythms. Travelers who jet from one continent to another have experienced discomforts that may last for days—until their bodies adjust to the new cycles. Perhaps these physiological disturbances will have to be paid for later in the form of pathological effects—we do not know yet, because the phenomenon is so new. We know that chickens will develop pathological symptoms if they are exposed throughout the year to artificial light for increasing egg production, but hardly anything is known of the effects produced in man by disturbances of his normal physiological rhythms.

In brief, there is no doubt that man is still immensely adaptable, but it is also certain he cannot adapt to just anything and everything. And the rate of his biological evolution is so slow that it cannot possibly keep pace with the rate of the technological and social change.

I don't deny that man has a remarkable capacity to adapt to new conditions. He has survived the horrible ordeals of modern warfare; he has multiplied in crowded and polluted cities; and he has worked effectively in atmospheres clouded by tobacco smoke and chemical fumes amid the infernal noise of telephones, typewriters and loud mechanical contrivances.

Because man adapted during evolutionary times to the vicissitudes of the Stone Age, it is often assumed that he can adapt now to all the traumatic conditions created by modern technology. But this is improbable. Conditions now exist that are without precedent in the biological history of man, and the chances are small that he is equipped to adapt to all of them.

Appetite

Immense progress has been made during the past century in the theory of nutrition and in the practical aspects of food production. But unfortunately, little is known of the kind of nutrition best suited to modern urban life. Nutritional requirements were determined two generations ago for vigorous and physically active young men, but these requirements do not necessarily fit automated, air-conditioned life. A new paradox is that the appetites our ancestors evolved to meet certain physiological needs may now be dangerous because strenuous physical exercise is no longer a part of everyday life.

Much remains to be learned about the nutritional needs of pregnant women and infants. The biggest baby is not necessarily the one that will be healthiest as an adult. Too generous a diet during early life may so imprint the child that his nutritional demands remain excessively large thereafter—deleterious effects in the long run.

Air

Environmental pollution provides another example of man's ability to function in a biologically undesirable environment, and also of the dangers inherent in this adaptability.

Since the beginning of the Industrial Revolution, inhabitants of Northern Europe have been exposed to a variety of air pollutants produced by coal and by the fumes from chemical plants, which are rendered even more objectionable by the inclemency of the Atlantic climate. But after long experience with pollution and with bad weather, Northern Europeans have developed physiological reactions and living habits that have adaptive value—they accept their dismal environment almost cheerfully. But even in those who seem to have adapted to irritating atmosphere, the respiratory system continuously registers the insult of air pollutants. As a result, chronic pulmonary disease is now the greatest single medical problem in

Great Britain. It is increasing at an alarming rate in North America, and it will probably spread to all areas undergoing industrialization.

There is evidence that air pollution increases the incidence of various types of cancers as well as the fatalities among persons suffering from vascular diseases.

Pattern

The delayed effects of air pollutants constitute models for the kind of medical problems that are likely to arise in the future from other forms of environmental pollution. People will insist that chemical pollution of air, water and food be sufficiently controlled to prevent immediately disabling and obvious toxic effects. But they will tolerate milder concentrations of environmental pollutants that do not interfere with social and economic life. Continued exposure to low levels of toxic agents will eventually result in a great variety of delayed pathology that will *not* be detected at the time of exposure and may not become evident *until several decades later.*

Noise is another aspect of environmental pollution that certain human beings come to tolerate, but at great cost. People adapt to continuous exposure to loud and painful noise by shutting out the objectionable sounds from perception. This, however, does not prevent destructive anatomical effects from taking place. There may be an impairment of hearing—a permanent inability to hear certain frequencies. The cost of adaptation to noise is therefore a loss in the enjoyment of music and of the more subtle qualities of the human voice.

Space

Adaptation to crowding may also have unfortunate results in the long run. Admittedly, man is a gregarious animal who commonly seeks crowded environments. But this does not mean that man can indefinitely increase the density of his populations; it means only that the safe limits are not known. In animals, crowding beyond a certain level results in behavioral and even physiological disturbances. Man has generally avoided the worst of these disturbances through a variety of social and architectural conventions and especially by learning to develop psychological unawareness of his surroundings.

In extremely crowded environments each of us lives—as it were—in a world of his own. But eventually this adaptation to crowding decreases man's ability to relate to other human beings. He may become unaware of their presence and totally antisocial.

Throughout prehistory and history, man has proved his ability to make adjustments that tend to correct the disturbing effects of the environment. Such adaptive responses contribute to the welfare of the organism at the time they occur, but may be deleterious at a later date. Many of man's chronic disorders are the secondary and delayed consequences of homeostatic responses that were adaptive at first but are faulty in the long run. For example, the production of scar tissue is a homeostatic response because it heals wounds and helps in checking the spread of infection. But when scar tissue forms in the liver or kidney, it means cirrhosis or nephritis; scar tissue may freeze the joints in rheumatoid arthritis or may choke the breathing process in the lung. In other words, homeostatic processes may have an immediate protective or reparative function, but they can become destructive in the long run. Wisdom of the body is often very short-sighted wisdom.

Mind

Adaptation can also be dangerous for mental health. Man seems to be adapting to the ugliness of smoky skies, polluted streams, and anonymous buildings; to life without the fragrance of flowers, the song of birds, and other pleasurable stimuli from nature. This adaptation, however, is only superficial, and destructive in the long run. Air, water, earth, fire, the subtle forces of the cosmos, the natural rhythms and diversity of life have shaped man's nature during the evolutionary past and have created deep-rooted sensual and emotional needs that cannot be eradicated. The impoverishment of sensual and emotional life will progressively result in the atrophy of our uniquely human attributes. Like the giant Antaeus in the Greek legend, man loses his strength when he loses contact with the earth.

Affluence

The greatest improvements in health during the past century have resulted from the continuous rise in our standards of living. But we may now be coming to the phase of diminishing returns. Our prosperity creates a new set of medical problems. Environmental pollution, excessive food intake, emotional deprivation, lack of physical exercise, the constant bombardment of unnatural stimuli, man's estrangement from natural biological rhythms—these are just some of the many consequences of urbanized and industrialized life that have direct or indirect pathological effects.

It can no longer be taken for granted that a further rise in living standards will continue to bring about improvements in health. More probably it will result in new patterns of diseases. Even if we can identify the factors responsible for chronic and degenerative diseases, it will prove extremely difficult to control them because all aspects of the urban and industrial environment are so intimately interwoven in the social fabric.

Freedom

Men will accept collective measures to protect the environment. Keeping streets and houses clear of refuse, filtering and chlorinating the water supplies, watching over the purity of food products, assuring a minimum of safe air in public places—these measures can be applied collectively, anonymously, and without interfering seriously with individual freedom.

But any measure that requires individual discipline and personal effort is likely to be neglected. Almost everybody is aware of the dangers associated with overeating, failure to engage in physical exercise, chain cigarette smoking, excessive consumption of drugs, constant exposure to pollution, noise and people. But few persons are willing to make the individual efforts necessary to avoid these dangers. And the consequences of environmental threats are so often indirect and delayed that the public is hardly aware of them.

Self

The mass diseases of the past were connected quite directly with the natural environment. But the chronic and degenerative diseases and the mental disorders of today are integrated in a much more complex way with the sociocultural environment. For this reason they are much less amenable to community-based control than are the nutritional and infectious diseases, and demand that greater emphasis be placed on the cooperation and interest of the individual person. It is therefore necessary to reformulate medical policies so that the public-health practices that emerged from 19th-Century science will be supplemented by more personal relationships between physician and patient.

We shall of course develop new medical procedures for the treatment of the chronic and degenerative diseases—including the mental ones—that constitute the chief health problems of technological societies. We shall also develop protective technologies against environmental insults. But if we depend exclusively on such defense measures, we shall increasingly behave like hunted creatures, running from one therapeutic or protective device to another, each more complex and more costly than the one before. We shall end by spending much of our energy defending ourselves against environmental threats of our own creation, while sacrificing thereby the values that make life worth living.

Man should not try to conform to the environment created by social and technological innovations; he should instead design environments really adapted to his nature. He should not be satisfied with palliative measures treating the effects of objectionable conditions, but instead change the conditions. Now that scientific technology has made us so powerful, and so destructive, we must try to imagine the kinds of surroundings and ways of life we desire, lest we end up with a jumble of technologies and countertechnologies that will eventually smother body and soul.

Projects

1. Familiarize yourself with the noise pollution laws in your city. List the inadequacies of these laws. Submit a report to your city council, urging revision of the laws. Or arrange an interview with a council member to discuss the laws and your suggested revisions.

2. Read scientific studies of the effects of overcrowding on laboratory animals. Write a paper discussing the implications that these studies might have for man. Be careful to distinguish between suggestion and fact.

3. Read René Dubos' book, *So Human an Animal* (Scribner, 1968).

Present an oral report of the book. Point out ways in which Dubos' thesis reinforces ideas presented in the selections included in this textbook.

4. Dubos, as others have, discusses the difficulty of accomplishing reforms that depend on individual discipline and personal effort. What motivations will prompt you to responsible individual action on environmental problems? Discuss these motivations with your class.

5. Litter is one environmental problem which the individual must help solve. With this in mind, contact a local elementary school teacher and arrange to present to her class a brief educational program on litter. With two or three of your classmates, research the problems associated with litter. [See *Not So Rich As You Think* by George R. Stewart (Houghton Mifflin Company, 1967). "Keep America Beautiful," organized in 1953, is also a useful source of information concerning litter.] Then organize your information, adapt it to your audience, and select appropriate visuals. Present your report to the elementary school class. Ask the teacher to criticize your presentation. Revise your materials and give them to the teacher for her use in subsequent classes.

Suggested Topics for Writing

1. Examine your own environment and isolate those "conditions which now exist that are without precedent in the biological history of man." Consider the kinds of biological adaptations these require of man. Write an imaginative essay describing the creature man would become were he to undergo sudden evolutionary change prompted by the present environment. How do you *feel* as you read over your description?

2. Take a searching look at your own community. What "environmental insults" do you observe? Outline the most dangerous insults and suggest the "protective technologies" required to remove them.

Exercises

1. Why has Dubos titled his essay "Man Overadapting"?

2. Dubos asserts that "Conditions now exist that are without prece-

dent in the biological history of man, and the chances are small that he is equipped to adapt to all of them." Compile a list of these conditions. Consider the adaptations man must make in order to live with them. Which of these seem to be dangerous adaptations?

3. Examine Dubos' statement, "Clearly our adaptive potentialities are not unlimited." Is the negative statement more effective than a positive statement would have been (for example, "Our adaptive potentialities are limited.")?

4. Examine the organization of Dubos' essay. At what point do his introductory remarks end and the body of the essay begin? How many main points make up the body of the essay? What kinds of evidence are introduced in support of each of the main assertions? What method has Dubos used to conclude his essay?

5. Define the following words used in the essay: microbial, ubiquitous, multiplicity, aberrations, vicissitudes, homeostatic, atrophy, pathological, and palliative.

6. What is the purpose of the analogy Dubos introduces as he discusses man's failure to respond successfully to modern ways of life. How effective is the analogy?

7. Explain in more detail the ways in which man is "intimately geared to the cosmic cycles."

8. At what rate does evolution in man occur? What is the difference between evolution and physiological adjustment? Is physiological adjustment always desirable?

9. Dubos writes not only of physiological adjustment which technological change has required of man, but also of mental and social adaptation it has necessitated. Discuss aspects of your immediate environment that have required biological, mental, and social adaptation because of changes occurring during the past ten years. To what degree are technological and social change dependent on one another?

10. Dubos is a professor and a member of the Rockefeller Institute. Remembering that he is a "scientist," consider his assertion that "The impoverishment of sensual and emotional life will progressively result in the atrophy of our uniquely human attributes." What other authors whose works are included in this text express similar views?

34. Eco-catastrophe!

PAUL EHRLICH

I

The end of the ocean came late in the summer of 1979, and it came even more rapidly than the biologists had expected. There had been signs for more than a decade, commencing with the discovery in 1968 that DDT slows down photosynthesis in marine plant life. It was announced in a short paper in the technical journal, *Science,* but to ecologists it smacked of doomsday. They knew that all life in the sea depends on photosynthesis, the chemical process by which green plants bind the sun's energy and make it available to living things. And they knew that DDT and similar chlorinated hydrocarbons had polluted the entire surface of the earth, including the sea.

But that was only the first of many signs. There had been the final gasp of the whaling industry in 1973, and the end of the Peruvian anchovy fishery in 1975. Indeed, a score of other fisheries had disappeared quietly from over-exploitation and various eco-catastrophes by 1977. The term "eco-catastrophe" was coined by a California ecologist in 1969 to describe the most spectacular of man's attacks on the systems which sustain his life. He drew his inspiration from the Santa Barbara offshore oil disaster of that year, and from the news which spread among naturalists that virtually all of the Golden State's seashore bird life was doomed because of chlorinated hydrocarbon interference with its reproduction. Eco-catastrophes in the sea became increasingly common in the early 1970's. Mysterious "blooms" of previously rare microorganisms began to appear in offshore waters. Red tides—killer outbreaks of a minute single-celled plant—returned to the Florida Gulf coast and were sometimes accompanied by tides of other exotic hues.

It was clear by 1975 that the entire ecology of the ocean was changing. A few types of phytoplankton were becoming resistant to chlorinated hydrocarbons and were gaining the upper hand. Changes in the phytoplankton community led inevitably to changes in the community of zooplankton, the tiny animals which eat the phytoplankton. These changes were passed on up the chains of life in the ocean to the herring, plaice, cod and tuna. As the diversity of life in the ocean diminished, its stability also decreased.

Other changes had taken place by 1975. Most ocean fishes that returned to fresh water to breed, like the salmon, had become extinct, their breeding streams so dammed up and polluted that their powerful homing instinct only resulted in suicide. Many fishes and shellfishes that bred in restricted areas along the coasts followed them as onshore pollution escalated.

By 1977 the annual yield of fish from the sea was down to 30 million metric tons, less than one-half the per capita catch of a decade earlier. This helped malnutrition to escalate sharply in a world where an estimated 50 million people per year were already dying of starvation. The United Nations attempted to get all chlorinated hydrocarbon insecticides banned on a worldwide basis, but the move was defeated by the United States. This opposition was generated primarily by the American petrochemical industry, operating hand in glove with its subsidiary, the United States Department of Agriculture. Together they persuaded the government to oppose the U.N. move—which was not difficult since most Americans believed that Russia and China were more in need of fish products than was the United States. The United Nations also attempted to get fishing nations to adopt strict and enforced catch limits to preserve dwindling stocks. This move was blocked by Russia, who, with the most modern electronic equipment, was in the best position to glean what was left in the sea. It was, curiously, on the very day in 1977 when the

Soviet Union announced its refusal that another ominous article appeared in *Science*. It announced that incident solar radiation had been so reduced by worldwide air pollution that serious effects on the world's vegetation could be expected.

II

Apparently it was a combination of ecosystem destabilization, sunlight reduction, and a rapid escalation in chlorinated hydrocarbon pollution from massive Thanodrin applications which triggered the ultimate catastrophe. Seventeen huge Soviet-financed Thanodrin plants were operating in underdeveloped countries by 1978. They had been part of a massive Russian "aid offensive" designed to fill the gap caused by the collapse of America's ballyhooed "Green Revolution."

It became apparent in the early '70s that the "Green Revolution" was more talk than substance. Distribution of high yield "miracle" grain seeds had caused temporary local spurts in agricultural production. Simultaneously, excellent weather had produced record harvests. The combination permitted bureaucrats, especially in the United States Department of Agriculture and the Agency for International Development (AID), to reverse their previous pessimism and indulge in an outburst of optimistic propaganda about staving off famine. They raved about the approaching transformation of agriculture in the underdeveloped countries (UDCs). The reason for the propaganda reversal was never made clear. Most historians agree that a combination of utter ignorance of ecology, a desire to justify past errors, and pressure from agroindustry (which was eager to sell pesticides, fertilizers, and farm machinery to the UDCs and agencies helping the UDCs) was behind the campaign. Whatever the motivation, the results were clear. Many concerned people, lacking the expertise to see through the Green Revolution drivel, relaxed. The population-food crisis was "solved."

But reality was not long in showing itself. Local famine persisted in northern India even after good weather brought an end to the ghastly Bihar famine of the mid-'60s. East Pakistan was next, followed by a resurgence of general famine in northern India. Other foci of famine rapidly developed in Indonesia, the Philippines, Malawi, the Congo, Egypt, Colombia, Ecuador, Honduras, the Dominican Republic, and Mexico.

Everywhere hard realities destroyed the illusion of the Green Revolution. Yields dropped as the progressive farmers who had first accepted the new seeds found that their higher yields brought lower prices—effective demand (hunger plus cash) was not sufficient in poor countries to keep prices up. Less progressive farmers, observing this, refused to make the extra effort required to cultivate the "miracle" grains. Transport systems proved inadequate to bring the necessary fertilizer to the fields where the new and extremely fertilizer-sensitive grains were being grown. The same systems were also inadequate to move produce to markets. Fertilizer plants were not built fast enough, and most of the underdeveloped countries could not scrape together funds to purchase supplies, even on concessional terms. Finally, the inevitable happened, and pests began to reduce yields in even the most carefully cultivated fields. Among the first were the famous "miracle rats" which invaded Philippine "miracle rice" fields early in 1969. They were quickly followed by many insects and viruses, thriving on the relatively pest-susceptible new grains, encouraged by the vast and dense plantings, and rapidly acquiring resistance to the chemicals used against them. As chaos spread until even the most obtuse agriculturists and economists realized that the Green Revolution had turned brown, the Russians stepped in.

In retrospect it seems incredible that the Russians, with the American mistakes known to them, could launch an even more incompetent program of aid to the underdeveloped world. Indeed, in the early 1970's there were cynics in the United States who claimed that outdoing the stupidity of American foreign aid would be physically impossible. Those critics were, however, obviously unaware that the Russians had been busily destroying their own environment for many years. The virtual disappearance of sturgeon from Russian rivers caused a great shortage of caviar by 1970. A standard joke among Russian scientists at that time was that they had created an artificial caviar which was indistinguishable from the real thing— except by taste. At any rate the Soviet Union, observing with interest the progressive deterioration of relations between the UDCs and the United States, came up with a solution. It had recently developed what it claimed was the ideal insecticide, a highly lethal chlorinated hydrocarbon complexed with a special agent for penetrating the external skeletal armor of insects. Announcing that the new pesticide, called Thanodrin, would truly produce a Green Revolution, the Soviets entered into negotiations with various UDCs for the construction of massive Thanodrin factories. The USSR would bear all the costs; all it wanted in return were certain trade and military concessions.

It is interesting now, with the perspective of years, to examine in some detail the reasons why the UDCs welcomed the Thanodrin plan with such open arms. Government officials in these countries ignored the protests of their own scientists that Thanodrin would not solve the problems which plagued them. The governments now knew that the basic cause of their problems was overpopulation, and that these problems had been exacerbated by the dullness, daydreaming, and cupidity endemic to all governments. They knew that only population control and limited development aimed primarily at agriculture could have spared them the horrors they now faced. They knew it, but they were not about to admit it. How much easier it was simply to accuse the Americans of failing to give them proper aid; how much simpler to accept the Russian panacea.

And then there was the general worsening of relations between the United States and the UDCs. Many things had contributed to this. The situation in America in the first half of the 1970's deserves our close scrutiny. Being more dependent on imports for raw materials than the Soviet Union, the United States had, in the early 1970's, adopted more and more heavy-handed policies in order to insure continuing supplies. Military adventures in Asia and Latin America had further lessened the international credibility of the United States as a great defender of freedom—an image which had begun to deteriorate rapidly during the pointless and fruitless Viet-Nam conflict. At home, acceptance of the carefully manufactured image lessened dramatically, as even the more romantic and chauvinistic citizens began to understand the role of the military and the industrial system in what John Kenneth Galbraith had aptly named "The New Industrial State."

At home in the USA the early '70s were traumatic times. Racial violence grew and the habitability of the cities diminished as nothing substantial was done to ameliorate either racial inequities or urban blight. Welfare rolls grew as automation and general technological progress forced more and more people into the category of "unemployable." Simultaneously a taxpayers' revolt occurred. Although there was not enough money to build the schools, roads, water systems, sewage systems, jails, hospitals, urban transit lines, and all the other amenities needed to support a burgeoning population, Americans refused to tax themselves more heavily. Starting in Youngstown, Ohio in 1969 and followed closely by Richmond, California, community after community was forced to close its schools or curtail educational operations for lack of funds. Water supplies, already marginal in quality and quantity in many places by 1970, deteriorated quickly. Water rationing occurred in 1723 municipalities in the summer of 1974, and hepatitis and epidemic dysentery rates climbed about 500 per cent between 1970–1974.

III

Air pollution continued to be the most obvious manifestation of environmental deterioration. It was, by 1972, quite literally in the eyes of all Americans. The year 1973 saw not only the New York and Los Angeles smog disasters, but also the publication of the Surgeon General's massive report on air pollution and health. The public had been partially prepared for the worst by the publicity given to the U.N. pollution conference held in 1972. Deaths in the late '60s caused by smog were well known to scientists, but the public had ignored them because they mostly involved the early demise of the old and sick rather than people dropping dead on the freeways. But suddenly our citizens were faced with nearly 200,000 corpses and massive documentation that they could be the next to die from respiratory disease. They were not ready for that scale of disaster. After all, the U.N. conference had not predicted that accumulated air pollution would make the planet uninhabitable until almost 1990. The population was terrorized as TV screens became filled with scenes of horror from the disaster areas. Especially vivid was NBC's coverage of hundreds of unattended people choking out their lives outside of New York's hospitals. Terms like nitrogen oxide, acute bronchitis and cardiac arrest began to have real meaning for most Americans.

The ultimate horror was the announcement that chlorinated hydrocarbons were now a major constituent of air pollution in all American cities. Autopsies of smog disaster victims revealed an average chlorinated hydrocarbon load in fatty tissue equivalent to 26 parts per million of DDT. In October, 1973, the Department of Health, Education and Welfare announced studies which showed unequivocally that increasing death rates from hypertension, cirrhosis of the liver, liver cancer and a series of other diseases had resulted from the chlorinated hydrocarbon load. They estimated that Americans born since 1946 (when DDT usage began) now had a life expectancy of only 49 years, and predicted that if current patterns continued, this expectancy would reach 42 years by 1980, when it might level out. Plunging insurance stocks triggered a stock market panic. The president of Velsicol, Inc., a major pesticide producer, went on television to "publicly eat a teaspoonful of DDT" (it was really powdered milk) and announce that HEW had been infiltrated by Communists. Other giants of the petrochemical industry, attempting to dispute the indisputable evidence, launched a massive pressure campaign on Congress to force HEW to "get out of agriculture's business." They were aided by the agro-chemical journals, which had decades of experience in misleading the public about the benefits and dangers of pesticides. But by now the public realized that it had been duped. The Nobel Prize for medicine and physiology was given to Drs. J. L. Radomski and W. B. Deichmann, who in the late 1960's had pioneered in the documentation of the long-term lethal effects of chlorinated hydrocarbons. A Presidential Commission with unimpeachable credentials directly accused the agro-chemical complex of "condemning many millions of Americans to an early death." The year 1973 was the year in which Americans finally came to understand the direct threat to their existence posed by environmental deterioration.

And 1973 was also the year in which most people finally comprehended the indirect threat. Even the president of Union Oil Company and several other industrialists publicly stated their concern over the reduction of bird populations which had resulted from pollution by DDT and other chlorinated hydrocarbons. Insect populations boomed because they were resistant to most pesticides and had been freed, by the incompetent use of those pesticides, from most of their natural enemies. Rodents swarmed over crops, multiplying rapidly in the absence of predatory birds. The effect of pests on the wheat crop was especially disastrous in the summer of 1973, since that was also the year of the great drought. Most of us can remember the shock which greeted the announcement by atmospheric physicists that the shift of the jet stream which had caused the drought was probably permanent. It signalled the birth of the Midwestern desert. Man's air-polluting activities had by then caused gross changes in climatic patterns. The news, of course, played hell with commodity and stock markets. Food prices skyrocketed, as savings were poured into hoarded canned goods. Official assurances that food supplies would remain ample fell on deaf ears, and even the government showed signs of nervousness when California migrant field workers went out on strike again in protest against the continued use of pesticides by growers. The strike burgeoned into farm burning and riots. The workers, calling themselves "The Walking Dead," demanded immediate compensation for their shortened lives, and crash research programs to attempt to lengthen them.

It was in the same speech in which President Edward Kennedy, after much delay, finally declared a national emergency and called out the National Guard to harvest California's crops, that the first mention of population control was made. Kennedy pointed out that the United States would no longer be able to offer any food aid to other nations and was likely to suffer food shortages herself. He suggested that, in view of the manifest failure of the Green Revolution, the only hope of the UDCs lay in population control. His statement, you will recall, created an uproar in the underdeveloped countries. Newspaper editorials accused the United States of wishing to prevent small countries from becoming large nations and thus threatening American hegemony. Politicians asserted that President Kennedy was a "creature of the giant drug combine" that wished to shove its pills down every woman's throat.

Among Americans, religious opposition to population control was very slight. Industry in general also backed the idea. Increasing poverty in the UDCs was both destroying markets and threatening supplies of raw materials. The seriousness of the raw material situation had been brought home during the Congressional Hard Resources hearings in 1971. The exposure of the ignorance of the cornucopian economists had been quite a spectacle—a spectacle brought into virtually every American's home in living color. Few would forget the distinguished geologist from the University of California who suggested that economists be legally required to learn at least the most elementary facts of geology. Fewer still would forget that an equally distinguished Harvard economist added that they might be required to learn some economics, too. The overall message was clear: America's resource situation was bad and bound to get worse. The hearings had led to a bill requiring the Departments of State, Interior, and Commerce to set up a joint resource procurement council with the express purpose of "insuring that proper consideration of American resource needs be an integral part of American foreign policy."

Suddenly the United States discovered that it had a national consensus: population control was the only possible salvation of the underdeveloped world. But that same consensus led to heated debate. How could the UDCs be persuaded to limit their populations, and should not the United States lead the way by limiting its own? Members of the intellectual community wanted America to set an example. They pointed out that the United States was in the midst of a new baby boom: her birth rate, well over 20 per thousand per year, and her growth rate of over one per cent per annum were among the very highest of the developed countries. They detailed the deterioration of the American physical and psychic environments, the growing health threats, the impending food shortages, and the insufficiency of funds for desperately needed public works. They contended that the nation was clearly unable or unwilling to properly care for the people it already had. What possible reason could there be, they queried, for adding any more? Besides, who would listen to requests by the United States for population control when that nation did not control her own profligate reproduction?

Those who opposed population controls for the U.S. were equally vociferous. The military-industrial complex, with its all-too-human mixture of ignorance and avarice, still saw strength and prosperity in numbers. Baby food magnates, already worried by the growing nitrate pollution of their products, saw their market disappearing. Steel manufacturers saw a decrease in aggregate demand and slippage for that holy of holies, the Gross National Product. And military men saw, in the growing population-food-environment crisis, a serious threat to their carefully nurtured Cold War. In the end, of course, economic arguments held sway, and the "inalienable right of every American couple to determine the size of its family," a freedom invented for the occasion in the early '70s, was not compromised.

The population control bill, which was passed by Congress early in 1974, was quite a document, nevertheless. On the domestic front, it authorized an increase from 100 to 150 million dollars in funds for "family planning" activities. This was made possible by a general feeling in the country that the growing army on welfare needed family planning. But the gist of the bill was a series of measures designed to impress the need for population control on the

UDCs. All American aid to countries with overpopulation problems was required by law to consist in part of population control assistance. In order to receive any assistance each nation was required not only to accept the population control aid, but also to match it according to a complex formula. "Overpopulation" itself was defined by a formula based on U.N. statistics, and the UDCs were required not only to accept aid, but also to show progress in reducing birth rates. Every five years the status of the aid program for each nation was to be re-evaluated.

The reaction to the announcement of this program dwarfed the response to President Kennedy's speech. A coalition of UDCs attempted to get the U.N. General Assembly to condemn the United States as a "genetic aggressor." Most damaging of all to the American cause was the famous "25 Indians and a dog" speech by Mr. Shankarnarayan, Indian Ambassador to the U.N. Shankarnarayan pointed out that for several decades the United States, with less than six per cent of the people of the world had consumed roughly 50 per cent of the raw materials used every year. He described vividly America's contribution to worldwide environmental deterioration, and he scathingly denounced the miserly record of United States foreign aid as "unworthy of a fourth-rate power, let alone the most powerful nation on earth."

It was the climax of his speech, however, which most historians claim once and for all destroyed the image of the United States. Shankarnarayan informed the assembly that the average American family dog was fed more animal protein per week than the average Indian got in a month. "How do you justify taking fish from protein-starved Peruvians and feeding them to your animals?" he asked. "I contend," he concluded, "that the birth of an American baby is a greater disaster for the world than that of 25 Indian babies." When the applause had died away, Mr. Sorensen, the American representative, made a speech which said essentially that "other countries look after their own self-interest, too." When the vote came, the United States was condemned.

IV

This condemnation set the tone of U.S.-UDC relations at the time the Russian Thanodrin proposal was made. The proposal seemed to offer the masses in the UDCs an opportunity to save themselves and humiliate the United States at the same time; and in human affairs, as we all know, biological realities could never interfere with such an opportunity. The scientists were silenced, the politicians said yes, the Thanodrin plants were built, and the results were what any beginning ecology student could have predicted. At first Thanodrin seemed to offer excellent control of many pests. True, there was a rash of human fatalities from improper use of the lethal chemical, but, as Russian technical advisors were prone to note, these were more than compensated for by increased yields. Thanodrin use skyrocketed throughout the underdeveloped world. The Mikoyan design group developed a dependable, cheap agricultural aircraft which the Soviets donated to the effort in large numbers. MIG sprayers became even more common in UDCs than MIG interceptors.

Then the troubles began. Insect strains with cuticles resistant to Thanodrin penetration began to appear. And as streams, rivers, fish culture ponds and onshore waters became rich in Thanodrin, more fisheries began to disappear. Bird populations were decimated. The sequence of events was standard for broadcast use of a synthetic pesticide: great success at first, followed by removal of natural enemies and development of resistance by the pest. Populations of crop-eating insects in areas treated with Thanodrin made steady comebacks and soon became more abundant than ever. Yields plunged, while farmers in their desperation increased the Thanodrin dose and shortened the time between treatments. Death from Thanodrin poisoning became common. The first violent incident occurred in the Canete Valley of Peru, where farmers had suffered a similar chlorinated hydrocarbon disaster in the mid-'50s. A Russian advisor serving as an agricultural pilot was assaulted and killed by a mob of enraged farmers in January, 1978. Trouble spread rapidly during 1978, especially after the word got out that two years earlier Russia herself had banned the use of Thanodrin at home because of its serious effects on ecological systems. Suddenly Russia, and not the United States, was the *bête noir* in the UDCs. "Thanodrin parties" became epidemic, with farmers, in their ignorance, dumping carloads of Thanodrin concentrate into the sea. Russian advisors fled, and four of the Thanodrin plants were leveled to the ground. Destruction of the plants in Rio and Calcutta led to hundreds of thousands of gallons of Thanodrin concentrate being dumped directly into the sea.

Mr. Shankarnarayan again rose to address the U.N., but this

time it was Mr. Potemkin, representative of the Soviet Union, who was on the hot seat. Mr. Potemkin heard his nation described as the greatest mass killer of all time as Shankarnarayan predicted at least 30 million deaths from crop failures due to overdependence on Thanodrin. Russia was accused of "chemical aggression," and the General Assembly, after a weak reply by Potemkin, passed a vote of censure.

It was in January, 1979, that huge blooms of a previously unknown variety of diatom were reported off the coast of Peru. The blooms were accompanied by a massive die-off of sea life and of the pathetic remainder of the birds which had once feasted on the anchovies of the area. Almost immediately another huge bloom was reported in the Indian ocean, centering around the Seychelles, and then a third in the South Atlantic off the African coast. Both of these were accompanied by spectacular die-offs of marine animals. Even more ominous were growing reports of fish and bird kills at oceanic points where there were no spectacular blooms. Biologists were soon able to explain the phenomena: the diatom had evolved an enzyme which broke down Thanodrin; that enzyme also produced a breakdown product which interfered with the transmission of nerve impulses, and was therefore lethal to animals. Unfortunately, the biologists could suggest no way of repressing the poisonous diatom bloom in time. By September, 1979, all important animal life in the sea was extinct. Large areas of coastline had to be evacuated, as windrows of dead fish created a monumental stench.

But stench was the least of man's problems. Japan and China were faced with almost instant starvation from a total loss of the seafood on which they were so dependent. Both blamed Russia for their situation and demanded immediate mass shipments of food. Russia had none to send. On October 13, Chinese armies attacked Russia on a broad front. . . .

V

A pretty grim scenario. Unfortunately, we're a long way into it already. Everything mentioned as happening before 1970 has actually occurred; much of the rest is based on projections of trends already appearing. Evidence that pesticides have long-term lethal effects on human beings has started to accumulate, and recently Robert Finch,

Secretary of the Department of Health, Education and Welfare expressed his extreme apprehension about the pesticide situation. Simultaneously the petrochemical industry continues its unconscionable poison-peddling. For instance, Shell Chemical has been carrying on a high-pressure campaign to sell the insecticide Azodrin to farmers as a killer of cotton pests. They continue their program even though they know that Azodrin is not only ineffective, but often *increases* the pest density. They've covered themselves nicely in an advertisement which states, "Even if an overpowering migration [sic] develops, the flexibility of Azodrin lets you regain control fast. Just increase the dosage according to label recommendations." It's a great game—get people to apply the poison and kill the natural enemies of the pests. Then blame the increased pests on "migration" and sell even more pesticide!

Right now fisheries are being wiped out by over-exploitation, made easy by modern electronic equipment. The companies producing the equipment know this. They even boast in advertising that only their equipment will keep fishermen in business until the final kill. Profits must obviously be maximized in the short run. Indeed, Western society is in the process of completing the rape and murder of the planet for economic gain. And, sadly, most of the rest of the world is eager for the opportunity to emulate our behavior. But the underdeveloped peoples will be denied that opportunity—the days of plunder are drawing inexorably to a close.

Most of the people who are going to die in the greatest cataclysm in the history of man have already been born. More than three and a half billion people already populate our moribund globe, and about half of them are hungry. Some 10 to 20 million will starve to death *this year*. In spite of this, the population of the earth will increase by 70 million souls in 1969. For mankind has artificially lowered the death rate of the human population, while in general birth rates have remained high. With the input side of the population system in high gear and the output side slowed down, our fragile planet has filled with people at an incredible rate. It took several million years for the population to reach a total of two billion people in 1930, while a *second two billion will have been added by 1975!* By that time some experts feel that food shortages will have escalated the present level of world hunger and starvation into famines of unbelievable proportions. Other experts, more optimistic, think the ultimate food-population collision will not occur until the decade of the 1980's. Of course more massive famine may be avoided if other events cause a prior rise in the human death rate.

Both worldwide plague and thermonuclear war are made more probable as population growth continues. These, along with famine, make up the trio of potential "death rate solutions" to the population problem—solutions in which the birth rate–death rate imbalance is redressed by a rise in the death rate rather than by a lowering of the birth rate. Make no mistake about it, *the imbalance will be redressed.* The shape of the population growth curve is one familiar to the biologist. It is the outbreak part of an outbreak-crash sequence. A population grows rapidly in the presence of abundant resources, finally runs out of food or some other necessity, and crashes to a low level or extinction. Man is not only running out of food, he is also destroying the life support systems of the Spaceship Earth. The situation was recently summarized very succinctly: "It is the top of the ninth inning. Man, always a threat at the plate, has been hitting Nature hard. It is important to remember, however, that NATURE BATS LAST."